The Changing American
Consumer

The Changing American Consumer

Marianne Bickle, PH.D.
in cooperation with the **Prosper Foundation**

The Changing American Consumer
by Marianne Bickle, Ph.D., in cooperation with the Prosper Foundation

ISBN 978-0-9819415-8-5

Library of Congress Control Number 2011943933

Printed in the United States of America

10 9 8 7 6 5 4 3 2 1

Published by Prosper Publishing
Website: www.goprosper.com

Prosper Publishing books are available at special quantity discounts to use for sales promotions, employee premiums, or educational purposes. To order or for more information, please call 614-846-0146 or write to Prosper Publishing, 400 West Wilson Bridge Road, Suite 200, Worthington, OH, 43085.

Cover and Interior Book Design by Sun Editing & Book Design (www.suneditwrite.com)

Disclaimer: This book provides general information that is intended to inform and educate the reader on a general basis. Every effort has been made to assure that the information contained herein is accurate and timely as of the date of publication. However, it is provided for the convenience of the reader only. THE AUTHORS, PUBLISHER AND ALL AFFILIATED PARTIES EXPRESSLY DISCLAIM ANY AND ALL EXPRESS OR IMPLIED WARRANTIES, INCLUDING THE IMPLIED WARRANTY OF MERCHANTABILITY AND FITNESS FOR A PARTICULAR PURPOSE. The information presented herein may not be suitable for each reader's particular situation. It is recommended that each reader consult a professional in the reader's respective discipline for further advice on this subject. Reliance on the information in this book is at the reader's sole risk. In no event, are the Authors, Publisher or any affiliated party liable for any direct, indirect, incidental, consequential or other damages of any kind whatsoever including lost profits, relative to the information or advice provided herein. Reference to any specific commercial product, process or service, does not constitute an endorsement or recommendation.

To
Melvina Mary Young and Pamela Ann Setla

Contents

Acknowledgements

An enormous amount of gratitude is extended to consumers nationwide who have responded to the BIGinsight™ surveys throughout the years. The data will help businesses better understand the changing consumer footprint. The excellent team at BIGinsight was instrumental in making this project come alive. They include, in alphabetical order, Stephanie Blakely, Gary Drenik, Randi Honkonen, Pam Goodfellow, Roger Saunders, Phil Rist, Stacie Severs, and Chrissy Wissinger. Chrissy was particularly instrumental in helping this book make it to the publisher. She spent untold hours editing and double checking data. Chrissy is patient beyond belief and cheerfully accepts the many drafts that come with writing a book.

Writing a book in one year takes an enormous amount of time. My family was very generous and understanding. Diane and Bill Bousquette were incredibly understanding when I kept saying, "I'm writing, I can't talk now," or "I need to cancel I'm under a deadline." My sister Pamela was a great supporter of the book. As a journalist, she was inquisitive about the writing process, without putting undue pressure on the outcome.

Finally, an enormous amount of thanks goes to Diane Brewer, Vickie Smith, Michele and Samuel Sullivan and Will and Susan Taylor.

Thank you for purchasing *The Changing American Consumer*. As part of your purchase, you have complimentary ongoing access to **The Changing American Consumer App and InsightCenter™**. This exciting service provides you with a direct link to the heart and mind of the American consumer.

The Changing American Consumer App and InsightCenter includes current insights explored in the book such as consumer confidence, employment outlook, financial wellbeing, home and auto purchase intentions and new media usage.

Plus as an added bonus, we've included additional insights not found in the book:

- At what gas prices do consumers make changes and what changes do they make?

- Purchase plans for computers and mobile devices are on the rise: How will this affect plans to buy stereo equipment and digital cameras?

- At what income level do American consumers feel like they are saving enough for their future needs?

The Changing American Consumer App and InsightCenter is updated on a monthly basis with responses from more than 8,000 adults. It highlights changing consumer sentiment and how it impacts purchasing behavior and motivators. Register today to meet the **New American Consumer!**

REGISTER TODAY!

www.ChangingConsumer.com

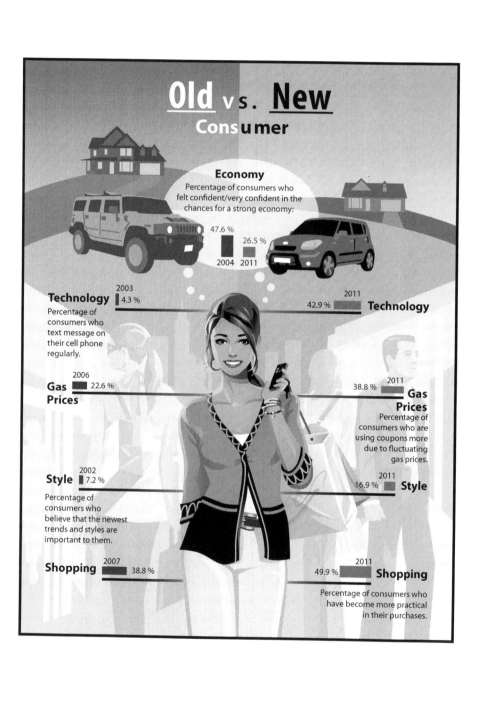

Old vs. New
Consumer

Economy
Percentage of consumers who felt confident/very confident in the chances for a strong economy:

47.6 %
26.5 %
2004   2011

Technology
2003
4.3 %
Percentage of consumers who text message on their cell phone regularly.

2011
42.9 %
Technology

Gas Prices
2006
22.6 %

38.8 %
2011
Gas Prices
Percentage of consumers who are using coupons more due to fluctuating gas prices.

Style
2002
7.2 %
Percentage of consumers who believe that the newest trends and styles are important to them.

16.9 %
2011
Style

Shopping
2007
38.8 %

49.9 %
2011
Shopping
Percentage of consumers who have become more practical in their purchases.

Foreword

We all know how radically 9/11 impacted American society. The long lines and heightened security measures at airports, and the talk of a national threat were just part of it all. The war on terror took America to lands far away, such as Afghanistan and Iraq, while at home there was a heightened sense of patriotism that even saw both parties in Congress working together. In the light of the tragedy, Americans everywhere began to reevaluate their personal priorities and wonder if the nation would ever be the same again.

The average consumer may have retreated initially, but soon returned—with a new attitude. A more practical approach to consumption, coupled with rapidly advancing technological changes, propelled new retailers to the forefront: Walmart, Target, Kohl's, Costco, eBay, and Amazon.

There is no doubt that the new American consumer holds the reins in a market that is increasingly driven by technology. If the old retailers could rely on "location, location, location," they certainly can't anymore. Now selling is much more linked with a well-implemented online strategy, using such tools as Facebook or Twitter. So the question for business today is how to know and influence the customers.

It's true that consumers have been evolving ever since shopping began, but the series of shocks to society in this century—terrorism, financial crises, and natural disasters—has changed them forever. I am pleased to say that BIGinsight, with its unique methods and analytics software, has been well placed to provide insights that accurately documents these changes and convert it into relevant information that can benefit the contemporary American consumer and retailer.

The *Changing American Consumer* details what these changes are—not just broadly but by income and age bracket, and month-by-month. Crucially, it proposes how this understanding can be used to reach the new consumer, who has created and is in control of today's ever-changing marketplace.

Gary Drenik
Founder & Trustee
The Prosper Foundation

Baby Boomers focus was on wants, not on needs

Chapter

1

credit
29% interest rate

America, Land of Plenty?
The Times Are Changing

Even before immigrants came to Ellis Island looking for a new life filled with bountiful opportunities, the United States of America had declared itself the "land of the free, home of the brave, land of plenty," and was residence to some extremely successful entrepreneurs. Since then, individuals and families such as the Johnson family (Johnson & Johnson), Sam Walton, Jimmy Dean (Jimmy Dean Sausages), Mary Kay Ash (Mary Kay Cosmetics), Martha Stewart, Leslie Wexner (Limited Brands), and Ralph Lauren have built their consumer product empires from the ground up. These individuals exemplified the American dream: that anyone could become successful and wealthy. People throughout the world believed that once they reached America, this dream could be a reality. One caveat, that was before September 11, 2001.

On that day, the unspeakable happened. The United States experienced the worst case of terrorism in its history. It was made even more horrific by being televised on every national and international news channel twenty-four hours a day. The images were ingrained in consumers' brains. It felt like the beginning of the end. American consumers experienced the end of feeling safe, the end of feeling secure, and definitely the end of prosperity. September 11 changed the landscape of the American consumer.

Do we have confidence in the economy?

Consumer confidence is critical to the wellbeing of an economy. The more confidence consumers feel toward the economy, the more likely they will shop, take vacations, spend money, and invest in the stock market. This spending activity generates much needed tax dollars. It is a cyclical action that also helps get politicians re-elected. When consumers believe that the economy is doing well, they typically vote for the incumbent. Businesses generate sales and profits, consumers get new "stuff," and politicians keep their jobs. Ah, everyone is happy.

Let's look at Figure 1.1 to see consumers' confidence in the economy. BIGinsight surveyed 8,000 consumers nationwide. The black line represents all consumers, while the white line represents consumers who had a household income of $75,000 or more. In July 2003, 39.1% of the population sampled was confident about the economy, and 47.9% of those who earned $75,000 or more were confident. This figure improved slightly as the years progressed. But take a look at July 2008. Confidence in the economy took a nosedive. An average of only 18.8% of consumers was confident about the economy, with only 19.9% of consumers earning over $75,000 expressing confidence. Despite politicians' statements on national television that we were "headed in the right direction," consumers weren't buying the stories. By July 2011, consumers expressed only a bit more confidence about the economy: 26.5% of all households and 30.7% of households earning $75,000 or more were confident or very confident regarding the economy. These statistics look better than 2008, but, of course, it also means that approximately three-fourths of the consumers surveyed had little or no confidence in the economy. No wonder Washington was in a frenzy for much of 2011.

FIGURE 1.1: Consumers' Confidence in the Economy

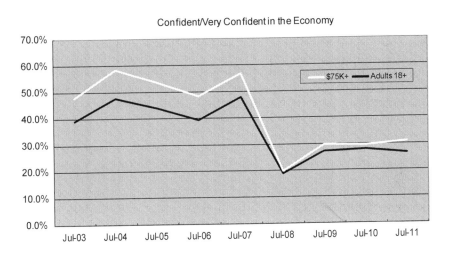

Source: BIGinsight.com

What do you mean my neighbor was laid off?

Another component of the economy and spending patterns was employment. After 9/11, news analysts (not just news anchors but elevated news analysts) talked about the economy. Consumers heard that the country was *entering* a recession. As time moved along, analysts changed their wording to state that America was *at the beginning phases of recession.* As one year turned into another year, *America was formally in a recession.* By then, news analysts and consumers alike talked about the country and how it was suffering another Great Depression.

Employment layoffs across the country were daily topics of conversation. It didn't matter if the company was large or small, from a rural community or a big city, employment downsizing made the front page. What was once considered a large employment sector was now viewed as small. Southern states experienced double-digit unemployment figures. Consumers regularly compared notes on family and friends in other states. Conversation revolved around questions regarding who had a job, who was laid off, who was about to be laid off. Meanwhile, there was speculation that the reported unemployment figures were low because many people had stopped getting unemployment checks or simply had given up.

Look at Figure 1.2. In July 2002, 7.8% of all households worried about layoffs. Concerns about job losses were not confined to consumers in lower income brackets. Of the households earning $75,000 or more, 12.2% worried about keeping their jobs. As consumers saw their neighbors get laid off, concerns increased. By July 2006, there was some breathing room. Businesses were doing a bit better and concerns regarding job security were a bit lighter. By July 2011, consumers were less nervous about joining the ranks of the unemployed. The really interesting statistic between July 2002 and July 2011 is that the consumers earning $75,000 or more annually felt more vulnerable about their jobs than did those earning less money. It is as if rising up the corporate ladder was no longer a guarantee of employment security.

FIGURE 1.2: CONCERNS REGARDING UNEMPLOYMENT

	Jul-02	Jul-03	Jul-04	Jul-05	Jul-06	Jul-07	Jul-08	Jul-09	Jul-10	Jul-11
Adults 18+	7.8%	6.2%	5.0%	4.0%	4.5%	4.0%	6.0%	7.9%	3.9%	3.6%
$75K+	12.2%	7.6%	5.5%	4.3%	5.3%	4.4%	7.0%	8.8%	4.5%	4.6%

Source: BIGinsight.com

Big bankrolls

The 1980s were characterized by big bankrolls and huge houses that were home to two-income families earning more than their parents could ever imagine, driving import luxury cars, and taking exotic vacations. Baby boomers built themselves a reputation of excess. Even their backyard clothes consisted of designer sweat pant suits accented by gold chains and diamond tennis bracelets.

Just like a roller coaster, what goes up must come down. The good times feeling came smashing down to earth along with everything else in the recession. After 9/11, suddenly having "all the good things" wasn't so good anymore. As it turned out, consumers were drowning in credit card debt. Jumbo mortgages and second and even third mortgages were crippling consumers' income flow when a spouse was laid off. The thought of saving for the future was just that—a thought. For many, the movie *Wall Street* epitomized the '80s, particularly Michael Douglas' character, Gordon Gekko, and his explicit "greed is good" attitude. Unfortunately, for the majority of us consumers, when we acquired shiny and pretty objects using credit, we weren't saving for our future needs.

Look at Figure 1.3. In August 2006, BIGinsight asked customers if they were saving for the future. Only 30.2% of all the consumers agreed and 45.0% of households earning $75,000 or more agreed that they were saving for the future. By February 2009, the number of consumers saving for the future declined: 24.9% of all households and 33.4% of households earning $75,000 or more were saving for the future. February 2011 revealed slight increases in consumers saving patterns but still lower than 2006.

The twenty-four-hour news cycle addressed the sad state of the economy. It provided consumers with an awareness of the lingering recession. Some would say that this information should have resulted in a greater number of consumers saving for the future. However, politicians' inability to fix double-digit unemployment throughout the country clearly impacted consumers' earning power. Rising prices for gas, food and clothing impeded combined with unemployment or paychecks that haven't risen in years contribute to consumers challenges in saving to meet future needs.

FIGURE 1.3: Consumers Saving for Future Needs

"I am saving enough to meet my future needs"
Agree/Strongly Agree

(chart showing $75K+ line and Adults 18+ line from Aug-06 to Feb-11, y-axis 0.0% to 50.0%)

Source: BIGinsight.com

Mama needs a new pair of shoes

If the '80s represented the philosophy that "more is better," it was also the era of placing *wants over needs*. No one really needed a new car every two years. The status of obtaining a car every two years, however, said, "I am successful and made a lot of money." Okay, so what if the car was a lease? So what if you were losing money on the car? Think about the enjoyment you got every time someone said, "Hey, is that a new car?" Who cares if you were shelling out $350 or more every month for the rest of your life? Think about the gratification you obtained from the new car smell.

Let's now fast-forward to 2002. It's as if consumers throughout America woke up from a very, very bad dream. The only problem was that it wasn't a bad dream. It was reality. Wait a minute! The guy who complimented you on the new car wasn't paying the car payment. The continual car payments—on not one but *two* cars—sucked the financial lifeblood out of the family wallet. Family *wants* all of sudden looked frivolous. You know the wants we are talking about: matching dirt bikes for the kids, a new set of golf clubs guaranteed to shrink the score, a premium gym membership that was used once a month—maybe… and the list went on. Individually the wants weren't all that expensive, or so it seemed. But add them all up each month and they made a staggering dent in an already fragile wallet.

The recession—if only consumers could forget about the recession. But the recession was only getting worse and getting bigger headlines in the news. No, sir! The tide had turned. The "me generation" of consumers woke up and changed their attitude. They took action and decided to *focus on their needs instead of wants.* They learned their lesson. Excess is bad. A survey of consumers during July 2003 revealed that 54.6% of all consumers surveyed said they placed needs before wants. Consumers who earned $75,000 or more also learned their lesson: 49.6% stated they now placed needs before wants.

Anyone who has ever graduated from high school has heard of Maslow's hierarchy of needs. Maslow stated that consumers satisfied their physiological needs first, which included food and shelter. The second set of needs to be satisfied was safety. The third type of needs was social (centered on love and belonging), followed by esteem, and finally, self-actualization. Check out Figure 1.4. Instead of reverting back to their old ways, an increased percentage of consumers in both groups (all consumers *and* consumers earning $75,000 or more) stated they focused on needs as opposed to wants. By July 2011, 58.5% of all consumers and 52.4% of consumers in households earning $75,000 or more focused on needs. These consumers focused on housing, food, and medical bills. The overt desire to display wealth was gone. The recession had changed consumers' attitudes toward consumption patterns. The question now to be answered is how will companies react to consumers' attitudes?

FIGURE 1.4: FOCUS ON NEEDS RATHER THAN WANTS

	Jul-03	Jul-04	Jul-05	Jul-06	Jul-07	Jul-08	Jul-09	Jul-10	Jul-11
Adults 18+	54.6%	54.0%	44.3%	52.0%	47.4%	58.1%	59.9%	58.0%	58.5%
$75K+	49.6%	46.7%	38.6%	48.6%	45.2%	56.7%	59.3%	53.6%	52.4%

Source: BIGinsight.com

Cash, credit, or debt?

It would be *so* easy to blame our actions on the state of today's economy. We could say that the terrorists of 9/11 made all the bad things happen to the economy. For example, after 9/11 the U.S. economy tanked. Well, this may be the simplest answer, but it is also not entirely correct. We will concede that many things went wrong after 9/11. However, history revealed that our economy and all it encompasses was heading for difficult times.

Prior to the '80s, anyone without a full-time job typically had a difficult time in obtaining a credit card. In those days, everything was paid for with cash. Cashing a check at a store required so many pieces of identification that it often wasn't worth the trouble. Then credit card companies realized that they were missing a very big target market, namely, the college student. By 2000, credit companies hit college campuses with a vengeance. Companies thought that parents would pay the outstanding balance. Once a student hit the limit on one card, another card was opened. It was "normal" for college students to have five credit cards.

Of course, consumers with jobs also hit the credit card scene hard. They played with credit card balances in a game of financial Russian roulette. When one company offered 0% interest on balance transfers, it was like a holiday, but somehow the credit card never got paid off and interest on new purchases kept adding up.

Look at Figure 1.5. Of the entire sample in July 2003, 29.9% said they were trying to pay more with cash, and 28.6% of the households earning $75,000 or more said the same. This trend continued as the recession dragged along. By July 2011, 24.4% of adults over eighteen tried to pay with cash, while 23.5% of the households earning $75,000 or more did the same. To a country addicted to plastic, these numbers were significant. Credit card debt across the U.S. was down as consumers realized that debt was not their friend. There was a very big difference between need and want and interest on a card makes a huge impact on the family budget.

FIGURE 1.5: DECISION TO PAY WITH CASH MORE OFTEN

	Jul-03	Jul-04	Jul-05	Jul-06	Jul-07	Jul-08	Jul-09	Jul-10	Jul-11
Adults 18+	29.9%	26.7%	22.7%	22.5%	19.7%	23.8%	25.3%	24.4%	24.4%
$75K+	28.6%	26.8%	23.5%	25.0%	20.7%	22.8%	24.4%	24.7%	23.5%

Source: BIGinsight.com

Summary

America is the land of the free, the home of the brave, and the land of plenty. Wait, scratch "land of plenty." America is land of the free and you really need to be brave in this economy. The recession hit hard and it hit deep. Consumers of all income brackets were impacted. Life as we knew it before 9/11 no longer exists. If you want to visit that lifestyle, read a book. Just don't go there for too long, you might get depressed.

The new millennium is a rough and tumble existence. Or maybe it simply means that we are going back to the basics. We as consumers are learning to live within our means, learning that more isn't always better, learning that our needs must be satisfied before we consider our wants, and learning to check our ego at the door when we shop. Saving money by using coupons, outlet shopping, and purchasing store brands is smart.

All lessons aren't necessarily easy to swallow. The lessons learned since 9/11 were financially driven and significant. With a little bit of luck, one day, America can go back to being the land of plenty. In the meantime, let's just keep progressing toward learning our lessons.

Top five lessons learned

1. The recession hit consumers hard, and only a quarter of consumers are confident about the economy.

2. Higher income wage earners worry more about being unemployed than do consumers earning less than $75,000 annually.

3. Most consumers are not prepared financially for the future.

4. Gone are the days of excess and satisfying our every desire. Consumers are thinking more about needs than wants.

5. Cash is king, debt is crippling, and credit will kill. An increased number of consumers are paying with cash.

Chapter

2

70% of us. economic activity is attributed to consumers

Consumers' Financial Wellbeing

There are two sides to every story. Some would say one side of the story is the truth, the other, fiction. It is simply the way you want to look at the story. If you want to feel all warm and fuzzy inside, then think of the best outcome no matter what the facts reveal.

In Chapter 1, we focused on one of the changing trends in America—the economy. Because the changes in the economy have such an enormous impact on consumers' attitudes and purchasing patterns, an entire chapter will be devoted to the subject. Of course, an entire series of books could be devoted to the economy. Just turn on the television. Cable news analysts discuss the economy 24/7. Perhaps at no other time in the past hundred years have consumers been so concerned with the economy, with the exception of the Great Depression.

What do you mean the economy is strong?

Perceptions matter—*a lot*. You may be thinking, "What makes consumers' perceptions so important to the economy?" Seventy percent of U.S. economic activity is attributed to consumers (Gross, Harris, & Murr, 2008). Think about it, over two-thirds of the health of the economy is down to consumer activity. When consumers spend and pay their debts, all is well. When consumers default on their debts, foreclose on the mortgage, and ignore creditors, havoc is wreaked on the economy.

In September 2011, we asked consumers to state their confidence regarding the economy. There were relatively little differences between consumers' opinions who earned $50,000 or more and the rest of the population. Take a look at Figure 2.1.

FIGURE 2.1: Consumers' Confidence for a Strong Economy

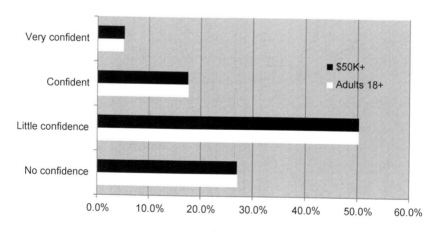

Source: BIGinsight.com

The year everyone would like to forget is 2008. It appears as if nothing good happened for businesses or consumers during that year. As it turns out, 2011 is also pretty bleak by consumers' standards: 77.3% of consumers earning $50,000 or more and 77.3% of all consumers have little or no confidence in a strong economy. It doesn't matter if you are making $20,000/annually or $50,000/annually consumer confidence in the economy is low.

I'm watching the bottom line

A comedian once said that there are two guarantees in life—death and taxes. The author would like to add a third guarantee. When the economy weakens, consumers tend to become budget conscious. Take a look at Figure 2.2.

FIGURE 2.2: PLANS TO SAVE COMPARED TO LAST YEAR

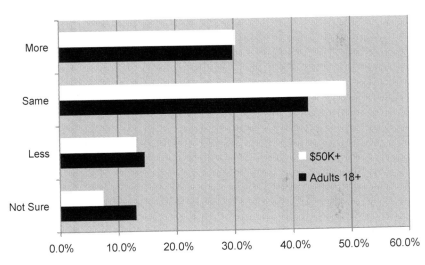

Source: BIGinsight.com

Sure enough, 30.4% of consumers earning $50,000 or more and 29.8% of all consumers decided that it was time to tighten their belts and save more than they did during 2010. It is interesting to note, however, that despite consumers' lack of confidence in the economy (as noted earlier); almost one half (49.2% and 42.6% respectively) were saving the same amount as the previous year. This could mean (a) the consumers had already tightened their budgets during 2010, (b) have absolutely no excess cash to save, or (c) are tired of saving and need a bit of "fun money."

The *not sure* group (7.3% earning $50,000 or more and 13.0% of all consumers) was the smallest group. Regardless of the state of the economy, saving for the future is always a wise plan. Financial counselors and financial self-help books can assist in helping the indecisive person better plan for the future. Someone very wise once told me that even if you saved $5 a month every month, it would be $60/year more than I was saving at the time. This concept seemed so simple.

Charge it x 2

Once upon a time, cash was king. Then, in 1950, Diners Club introduced the first credit card. Looking back sixty years, this innovative credit card looks interesting and exciting. Who knew it would permanently change the footprint of consumer spending patterns and the way businesses accepted payment. As credit cards became more widely adopted, consumers fell smack dab in the middle of a rollercoaster, passionate love affair with financial institutions. The affair can at times be very steamy and consumers can't get enough of the plastic. Vacations, business travel, holidays, birthdays, and special events are all good reasons to pull out the card and burn up the credit limit.

Like most relationships, there are two sides. Credit card companies aggressively woo, entice, and encourage consumers to adopt and use their cards. Credit cards come from a wide variety of sources: Visa, MasterCard, Diners Club and American Express are all popular credit card companies. So popular that, by the end of 2010, 181 million U.S. consumers were expected to possess a credit card.

Credit cards mean big business. Of course, like all business, it also brings risk. As we all know, once consumers purchase the goods or services using a card, they have to pay the credit card company. If the payment is only partially paid by the end of the month, an interest penalty is given. During difficult economic times, consumers are unable or unwilling to carefully estimate their spending patterns. By 2008, U.S. consumer credit card debt reached $951 billion. During 2009, credit card companies lost an estimated $75 billion in credit-card defaults (Stephey, 2009).

Store credit cards are very popular with large retailers. Target, Neiman Marcus, Nordstrom, and Bloomingdale's are examples of retailers that offer a store credit card. The store card offers consumers special discounts while enticing them to shop primarily at the retailer. What is so fascinating about the entire topic is the number of credit cards consumers possess. After all, credit cards don't offer free money. Some credit cards charge up to 22% interest on unpaid balances.

So, let's look at the credit card owners. We asked consumers which major credit cards they have. They were to list all the credit cards—hence, the percentages would be greater than 100%. Check out Figure 2.3. We found three interesting realizations. In September 2011, 66.2% of the respondents in household incomes earning $50,000 or more and 53.9% of all respondents possessed a Visa card. The credit card company's tagline during 2011 was, "More people go with Visa." According to this study, they are absolutely correct! Second, was MasterCard's popularity among respondents, it was second only to Visa, with 52.4% of respondents in household incomes earning $50,000 or more and 40.4% of all consumers possessing a MasterCard. MasterCard's tagline, "There are some things money can't buy, for everything else there's MasterCard," led us to our third realization. As we looked at percentages across the different credit cards and pondered MasterCard's tagline, the authors realized that the consumers also believed that, "One is not enough."

Reasons for multiple cards may include financial incentives, credit limits, trying to improve a credit rating, or multiple persons in a family. Regardless of the reasons, the possession of different credit cards is very popular.

FIGURE 2.3: CREDIT CARDS OWNERS

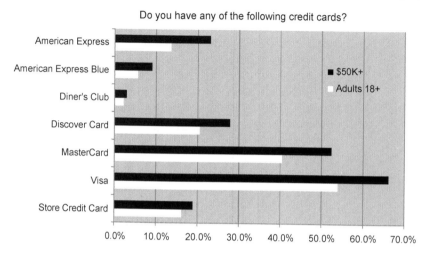

Source: BIGinsight.com

The many benefits of credit

Okay, so we know there are a lot of credit card offerings in the market-place. We also know that on average consumers possess more than one credit card. Consumers also have a lot of credit card debt. History has shown us that many consumers open up additional credit cards when existing accounts get maxed out.

The credit card industry, indeed most financial industries, is a highly competitive one. Successful companies don't sit back and wait for consumers to knock on their door. Guerrilla marketing techniques are used. Consumers are wooed, enticed, petted, and sometimes even bribed—legally bribed, of course.

We have always thought that any credit card company's unofficial motto is the company with the most active credit card accounts wins. During the late 1990s and early 2000s, credit card companies would offer 0% interest on all transfer balances to new customers. Instead of decreasing consumer debt, some consumers would transfer the balance, keep the existing account, and then rack up high debt on both cards.

The 0% balance transfer worked for a while. But credit card companies needed to reach out to more consumers. Let's not forget the motto: the company with the most active credit card accounts wins. This means the company can't lose any customers *and* customers need to use their credit card.

The most recent method of increasing consumer credit card loyalty and activity is through benefits. Consumers are now given a wide variety of possible benefits simply for using a credit card. Examples include discounts, cash back, airline miles, and rewards or points to purchase items. We asked consumers which benefits would motivate them to use a credit card more. Take a look at Figure 2.4.

We identified six different benefits offered by credit card companies: lower interest, discounts, cash back, airline miles, free shipping, and rewards or points programs.

Consumers in households earning $50,000 were motivated the most by cash back (52.6%), lower interest (45.7%), and rewards or points programs (39.8%). All consumers were also motivated by the same benefits but to a lesser degree (46.9%, 47.8%, 35.9% respectively). Discounts were somewhat important for both groups (32.5%, 31.8% respectively).

FIGURE 2.4: MOTIVATIONS TO USE A CREDIT CARD

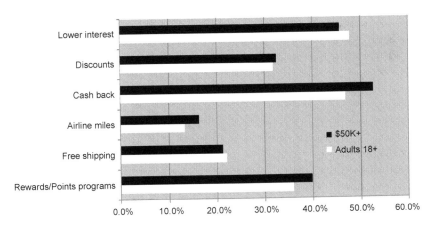

Source: BIGinsight.com

Four magic numbers

First, there was cash. If you didn't have cash to pay for products or service, maybe you could barter or trade. Then credit cards were invented. Many consumers adopted the belief that if you didn't have cash, credit cards were the perfect solution. Pay for the items at the end of the month. Or better yet, use the monthly installment plan. Okay, so you needed to pay 21% interest. You'd pay it off. Don't worry.

Now, we have a third option; the debit card. Consumers can use a debit card instead of writing a check. The debit card can also be used to get cash. What an invention! The banks love the debit card because it keeps consumers connected to the financial institutions. The ATM fees also generate income for the banks. Consumers love the debit card because of convenience. No more writing checks or need to carry around a lot of cash. To use the debit card, you simply need a checking card and four magic digits—your personal identification number, your PIN.

We decided to find out just how many consumers really do like using a debit card. Check out Figure 2.5.

FIGURE 2.5: Debit Card Use

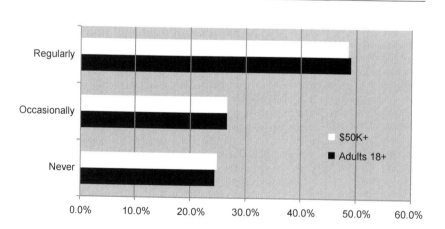

Source: BIGinsight.com

In September 2011 we asked our consumers how frequently they used their debit card. Of the group earning $50,000 or more, 48.5% used a debit card regularly, while 49% of all respondents used a debit card regularly. The percentages of respondents who never or occasionally used a debit card are relatively comparable.

Coming up for air

Being in debt is no way to walk through life. Being in debt during an economic recession when banks don't want to lend money is *really* no way to walk through life. The big spending days of the late twentieth century and first part of this century have put many consumers into a tailspin. They possess a lot of debt, and many have been either downsized with a smaller paycheck, laid off, have concerns of being laid off, or are worried about the future.

We asked consumers about their intensions regarding paying down their debt. Take a look at Figure 2.6. The survey revealed that 47.4% of consumers earning $50,000 or more and 34.3% of all consumers paid the balance in full each month. They obviously believed that if they wanted to be blood donors, they'd give to the Red Cross instead of the credit card companies.

In the beginning of the chapter, we mentioned that in 2008 U.S. credit card debt reached $951 billion. Some of the consumers responding to the survey helped contribute to this debt. That's because 40.9% of consumers earning $50,000 or more and 40.4% of all consumers who responded admitted carrying a credit card balance. With interest rates up in the 21% stratosphere, it doesn't take much to rake up high finance charges.

It is important to point out that some consumers either can't get credit or cut their credit cards up. Thus, 11.8% of those earning $50,000 or more and 25.3% of all consumers live their lives using cold, hard cash. Consumers using cash may be a group who (a) have learned that they cannot live a financially successful life with credit cards, (b) are able to purchase large items with a checkbook and don't need or want the temptation of a credit card or (c) are unable to obtain a credit card. The news and economy definitely suggest that consumers throughout the U.S. are trying to "come up for air." In a time when the economy is struggling, paying down debt may be a slow process. Fewer consumers are able to pay down the debt. They are taking financial steps one at a time.

FIGURE 2.6: CREDIT CARD PAYMENT SCHEDULE

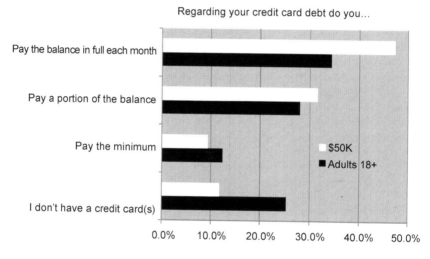

Source: BIGinsight.com

Stuff the mattress

When economic times are tough, consumers often think about the savings account. Consumers try to save money in this period because they are worried about the future. They pull money from the savings account because they are short on funds due to layoffs, unexpected expenses, or a "need" to spend.

We looked at consumers' intentions to increase savings in September 2011. As you can see in Figure 2.7, consumers were in a savings frame of mind: 49.2% of consumers earning $50,000 or more and 42.6% of all consumers planned to keep saving just as in 2010. An additional 30.4% of consumers earning $50K+ and 29.8% of all consumers stated that they were planning to save more than they did in 2010.

It would be logical to think that consumers with a household income of $50,000 or higher would increase savings, particularly during an economic recession. Bad things can happen to consumers in all income brackets. Unemployment, layoffs, medical problems, family issues, and an unsteady economy in general can influence consumers' ability to save. Also remember that regardless of income, everyone's ability to save is influenced by debt and inflation. Consumers across the nation were faced with rising gas, food and clothing prices. Quick assumptions can't readily be made that it is easier for one group to save than another. What can be noted is that consumers understand the importance of saving regardless of their income.

FIGURE 2.7: SAVINGS PLAN COMPARED TO LAST YEAR

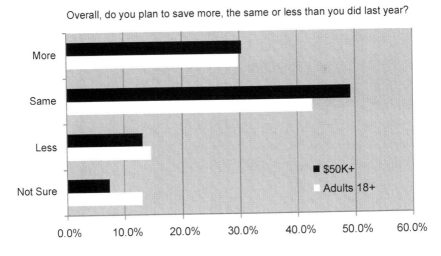

Overall, do you plan to save more, the same or less than you did last year?

Source: BIGinsight.com

The golden years

If you are over the age of fifty, you may relate to the following story. Once upon a time, people went to work five days a week. They worked very hard. When they reached the age of sixty-five, they were rewarded for their hard work. They retired. This retirement consisted of living in a home that was paid in full, taking vacations, playing golf or bridge, and generally living the good life. Money was not a problem because they had a retirement package and a savings account. Social security also helped cover general expenses.

The majority of consumers today can't retire when they are sixty-five. You may ask why. The answer, of course, is finances. The future is a funny thing. When we were all in our twenties, we were carefree and everything seemed possible. Then, with the blink of an eye somehow we are in our fifties and our hair is graying. Time passes very fast and it doesn't care if we are ready for the changes. Some of the changes are positive. Unfortunately, many of the recent economic changes have been negative and downright scary.

In September 2011 we asked consumers about their attitudes to saving for future needs. Look at Figure 2.8. We found that 31.5% of consumers in households earning $50,000 or more were uncertain if they were saving enough for future needs. An additional 35.8% of this group disagreed or strongly disagreed. In other words, 67.3% of consumers in household earning $50,000 or more had cause for financial concern regarding their future.

When we looked at all consumers over the age of eighteen, the financial future did not look any rosier. Almost 30% were uncertain and an additional 44.6% disagreed or strongly disagreed that they were saving enough for future needs. That is 73.8% of all consumers did not think they were saving enough for future needs.

Look at any big box store and you will realize that consumers across America have been unable to save enough money to retire. Consumers over the age of sixty-five are going back to work in secondary positions at an unprecedented rate. Not because they want to fill their time, because they want to fill their savings account.

FIGURE 2.8: CONSUMERS' SAVING FOR FUTURE NEEDS

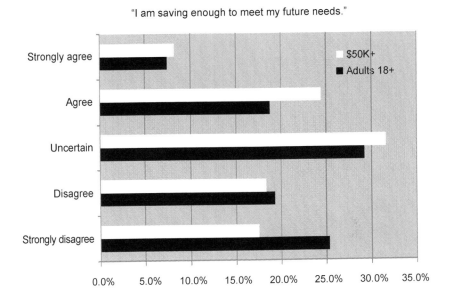

"I am saving enough to meet my future needs."

Source: BIGinsight.com

Summary

resilient ধैर्यवान अडिग

The government and consumers alike found out the hard way that what goes up must eventually come down. Housing prices, the number of jobs, and the willingness to save gave consumers and politicians a reality check when the recession hit. While the U.S. likes to consider itself a positive, strong, and resilient nation, the recession during the new millennium has shaken many consumers and businesses to the core. The way we view the economy may never be the same.

Top five lessons learned

1. The weakened economy is influencing consumers to become more budget conscious.

2. Consumers appreciate credit cards — if one credit card is good, two is better. Visa is the most popular credit card.

3. There are many reasons consumers are motivated to use credit cards more often. The three top reasons are lower interest rates, cash back, and rewards or points programs.

4. Debt is a national way of life. Consumers' strive to pay down debt, while less than 30% intend to increase their savings.

5. Consumers are retiring later in life.

References

Castro, J. and G. Bolte. "Charge It Your Way." *Time* (July 1, 1991) 50–51.

Devin, L. "The New Abnormal." *Bloomberg Businessweek* 4190 (August 2, 2010) 50–55.

Gross, D., A. Harris and A. Murr. "The Economy Sucks. But Is It '92 Redux?" *Newsweek* Vol 151, 3 (January 21, 2008) 52–53.

Smith, A. K. "It's the Debt Thing." *U.S. News & World Report* Vol. 130, 7 (February 19, 2001) 40.

Stephey, M. J. "A Brief History of Credit Cards." *Time* Vol 173, 17 (May 4, 2009) 16.

Chapter

3

Home Ownership:
Building the American Castle

The American dream has always been to have a home, a house, an abode. Whatever you call it, your residence represented stability, maturity, and financial growth. At the end of a long day in the trenches, Americans always counted on relaxing at home. However, the economic meltdown during the new millennium changed this scenario. Most Americans were grateful to be at work not sitting on the porch at home. Being at work meant you (a) were employed, (b) earned money to help pay for the jumbo mortgage payment you couldn't afford in the first place, (c) avoided looking at all the "stuff" inside your jumbo mini-castle that was paid using a credit card, or (d) avoided — at least temporarily — foreclosure on your house of the sort that had plagued your neighbors.

The American dream of homeownership has changed significantly over the last decade. The economy turned homeownership upside down. Grown children were no longer financially better than their parents. Home ownership was no longer an easy acquisition. So let's look at the changes in the American dream.

Welcome to my castle

Home ownership has always been a part of the American dream. Ever since Ozzie and Harriet welcomed us into their home, owning a home was as American as peanut butter and jelly. Since the 1950s, size mattered. Bigger was better. We were accustomed to the notion of supersize. Fast food meals were supersized as part of a value concept. Bundled staple products (socks, six for $3.00) were recognized as quality *and* quantity. Cars were transformed into SUVs. It was logical that consumers wanted giant-size homes.

Homes grew in size, making them miniature castles. The number of persons living in the home was irrelevant. What mattered was the square footage and amenities. Granite tile kitchen counter tops, stainless steel appliances, 50" flat-screen TV, and a three-car garage meant you had officially arrived. You had a mini-castle.

We decided to look at the trend toward homeownership. Check out Figure 3.1. We asked consumers if they owned a home. We then separated the group into two segments: all consumers over the age of eighteen; and consumers in households earning $75,000 or more. Between July 2002 and July 2011, all consumers over the age of eighteen fluctuated slightly in home ownership; overall, however the percent of consumers owning a home remained the same. In 2002, 60.5% of all consumers owned a home. By 2011, home ownership in this group remained relatively steady (59.8%). As we look at households where the income was $75,000 or more, the percent of consumers that owned a home ranged from 77.1% in July 2002 to 83.4% in 2011. Homeownership continues to play a dominant role in the American landscape.

FIGURE 3.1: PERCENT OF HOMEOWNERS

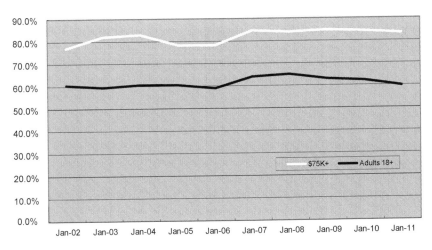

Source: BIGinsight.com

Blackjack or Go Fish: What's your level of risk?

Everything is different since 9/11. Let's list a few changes in the housing industry:

- Housing foreclosures are at an all-time high. *strangle. it*

- Families are declaring bankruptcy at an alarming rate, leaving their homes, and trying to start over.

- The once sought-after status symbol of a huge home is now an albatross around the consumer's neck—strangling them with debt.

- Two and three mortgages on a home are more common than any other time in history.

- The very popular five-year adjustable rate mortgage (ARM) has been replaced by a fixed-rate mortgage.

albatross

- Banks have turned off the flow of easy lending, and consumers are finding it increasingly difficult to obtain a home loan as a result of the nationwide economic meltdown.

Let's talk more about the five-year ARM. Before 9/11, interest rates were somewhat predictable and the economy was more stable. Employed consumers generally felt confident that they would be employed the following week. People who were going to be fired could read the writing on the wall. They either knew their company was in financial trouble or they knew one too many mistakes at work was ending the working relationship.

Then, one very awful day, everything seemed to change. What we didn't know (or didn't want to know) was that the banks would also fall along with the twin towers. Let's face it; did you ever think that banks would even whisper the words "We are failing"? Instead of keeping their failure secret, banks went to Capitol Hill and talked about it on television.

Such news combined with economic distress sent interest rates on a roller coaster. One day, rates were up, the next, they were down. The uncertainty of it was only for the strongest of stomachs. Fixed rate mortgages soon became more popular because the interest rate is predictable.

In the midst of the recession, we asked consumers if they had a fixed rate mortgage. We segmented the consumers into two groups: all homeowners over the age of eighteen; homeowners with an income of $75,000 or more. As you can see in Figure 3.2 consumers regardless of income or age overwhelmingly choose a fixed rate mortgage. For the most part, the percentage of consumers over the age of eighteen who had a fixed-rate mortgage remained relatively stable between July 2005 and July 2011. In July 2005, the majority of adults over the age of eighteen (84.9%) financed their homes with a fixed-rate mortgage. This figure was not surprising. By July 2011, the percent of consumers who needed a secured and fixed mortgage rose to 91.9%.

Now look at consumers in households where the income was $75,000 or more. In July 2005, 82.3% of those consumers had a fixed-rate mortgage. The percentage of consumers with this type of mortgage steadily increased throughout the years. News of the economy, rocky climate of the stock market, and downgrading of the economy all had its impact on wealthier consumers' mortgage decision. By July 2011, 92.4% of consumers in households earning $75,000 or more had a fixed-rate mortgage.

The statistics on this table reveal two important trends. Regardless of consumers' household income, 2011 was the year for fixed-rate mortgages and being careful to avoid gambling with interest rates. The old saying "It takes money to make money," may be adapted to "It takes money to save money."

FIGURE 3.2: CONSUMERS WITH A FIXED-RATE MORTGAGE

	Jul-05	Jul-06	Jul-07	Jul-08	Jul-09	Jul-10	Jul-11
Adults 18+	84.9%	82.6%	86.6%	89.6%	90.8%	89.3%	91.9%
$75K+	82.3%	81.4%	81.8%	81.6%	83.0%	85.4%	92.4%

Source: BIGinsight.com

I'm interested

A home is without a doubt the largest investment and financial debt most American consumers have undertaken. The majority of consumer mortgages are written for a thirty-year lifespan. This translates into paying interest on a very large mortgage for thirty long years. Between July 2002 and July 2011, interest rates on mortgages shifted as the economy shifted. We asked consumers if they refinanced their home. We looked at two groups: all consumers aged eighteen years and older; and consumers in households earning $75,000 or more.

July 2002 was a particularly active year for refinancing mortgages. Figure 3.3 reveals that 4.3% of all consumers refinanced their homes, while 7.7% of those earning $75,000 or more refinanced. Another active year was 2003, when 7.4% of consumers refinanced their homes, with 15.9% of those earning $75,000 or more refinancing.

These statistics are significant in the fact that it clearly shows that consumers with higher incomes refinanced their homes for a more favorable interest rate to a greater degree than did the rest of consumers. Once again, we are reminded of the lesson that money was required to save money.

During 2010 and 2011, mortgage interest rates became more favorable than in the previous years. Why didn't consumers in lower-income households (those under $75,000) refinance? Numerous reasons may be attributed to these results:

- Bad debt

- Unemployment

- Fear about not being able to obtain refinancing

- Not qualified because the new job does not pay as much as before

- House was in foreclosure

- Overwhelmed by the economy—becoming immobile on financial issues (translation: fear)

- Thought it wasn't worth the effort

Regardless of the reasons, consumers earning $75,000 or more took their finances in their own hands to a greater degree and refinanced their homes.

FIGURE 3.3: CONSUMERS PLANNING TO REFINANCE A HOME

	Jul-02	Jul-03	Jul-04	Jul-05	Jul-06	Jul-07	Jul-08	Jul-09	Jul-10	Jul-11
Adults 18+	4.3%	7.4%	3.0%	3.4%	2.6%	3.0%	2.6%	3.9%	3.9%	2.7%
$75K+		7.7%	15.9%	4.4%	6.0%	4.1%	4.5%	3.5%	7.4%	7.3%	5.0%

Source: BIGinsight.com

Who signs on the dotted line? *testosterone*

Blue is for boys and pink is for girls. Well, maybe not. I've seen some great looking guys in pink Ralph Lauren shirts. It also doesn't require testosterone or a wedding band to sign on the dotted line of a mortgage contract. Consumers prior to 1960 may have thought so but this is the new millennium. A sense of freedom is in the air. Besides, if it were up to only married couples to purchase homes, the real estate market would probably be in a panic.

We looked at gender and home ownership. Between July 2002 and July 2011, we examined which gender was more prone to own a home. Gender made a difference—as might be expected. As you look at Figure 3.4, you will notice that between July 2002 and 2011, women consistently were the primary homeowners.

FIGURE 3.4: HOMEOWNERS

	Jul-02	Jul-03	Jul-04	Jul-05	Jul-06	Jul-07	Jul-08	Jul-09	Jul-10	Jul-11
Male	46.5%	45.1%	45.9%	45.1%	44.0%	46.3%	47.4%	45.7%	47.1%	46.9%
Female	53.5%	54.9%	54.1%	54.9%	56.0%	53.7%	52.6%	54.3%	52.9%	53.1%

Source: BIGinsight.com

Okay, I'll admit that the statistics reveal that there was less than a 10% difference throughout the years. However, women continued to be the primary purchaser of homes. The reasons may have been due to the changes in the consumers' social background, such as:

- Increased numbers of women in the workforce,

- Increased divorce rate, whereby women get ownership of the marital home, or

- Increased access to loans during the 1990s.

Regardless of the reason, women are clearly a large target market for the housing industry, and certainly can no longer be ignored or assigned to the kitchen.

Breaking all the rules

Prior to 1970, the unofficial rule was that a couple would date, get married, and then buy a house. Times have changed. Homeownership is no longer reserved for life after the matrimonial bands have been shared. We examined the marital status of consumers between July 2002 and July 2011. Take a look at Figure 3.5.

Between July 2002 and 2011, over 61% of the consumers who were married owned a home. The percentage of consumers ranged from a high of 67.8% in 2002 to a low of 61.6% in July 2011. This relatively small fluctuation may be attributed to consumers staying together through necessity. As the recession raged on, staying in a less than perfect marriage solved the housing problem that would often arise after a divorce.

An interesting trend in homeownership is the percent of single, never married consumers who own a home. Between July 2002 and July 2011, singles flocked to the housing market. In July 2002, only 8.2% of single consumers owned a home. By July 2011, this figure rose to 15.6%. Lenders eased borrowing regulations, foreclosures offered good deals to first-time homebuyers, and the housing market nationwide was flooded with places that owners couldn't sell. All this translated into deep discounts for consumers wanting to buy homes.

Now look at the divorced or separated category. The marriage rate is 6.8 per 1,000 of the total population. The divorce rate in the U.S. was 3.4 per 1,000 (CDC, 2010). If you are part of the 50% of the American population that hasn't been divorced or separated, perhaps you don't understand the relatively low home ownership figures. Let us fill in all the fortunate happily married couples and single readers. Even under the best of circumstances, a separated or divorced couple divides their assets fifty-fifty. This arrangement could set the couple back financially anywhere from three to thirty years, depending upon the amount of assets, the ability to earn money, and state of the divorce (amicable or acrimonious).

In July 2002, 11.1% of the divorced or separated consumers stated that they were homeowners. Homeownership for this group fluctuated slightly, ranging from a high in July 2003 (12.5%) to a low in July 2010 (9.7%). A lot of variables may have influenced homeownership within this group: age, geographical location, how soon they divorced. The July 2010 statistic was not surprising. During 2010 and 2011, rentals and apartments became very popular as the economy became increasingly unstable. With very little money down, apartment living can offer the divorced or widowed flexibility, amenities, and even a social group (for example, in retirement apartments).

FIGURE 3.5: MARITAL STATUS OF HOME BUYERS

	Jul-02	Jul-03	Jul-04	Jul-05	Jul-06	Jul-07	Jul-08	Jul-09	Jul-10	Jul-11
Married	67.8%	66.8%	66.5%	66.2%	66.6%	65.3%	64.6%	65.7%	63.6%	61.6%
Living with partner	6.9%	6.4%	7.0%	7.0%	6.7%	5.8%	6.4%	6.0%	5.4%	6.4%
Divorced or separated	11.1%	12.5%	10.5%	10.8%	10.8%	10.1%	10.2%	10.1%	9.7%	10.2%
Widowed	6.0%	6.0%	6.0%	6.2%	6.9%	5.8%	5.9%	6.0%	6.1%	6.2%
Single, never married	8.2%	8.3%	10.0%	9.9%	9.0%	12.9%	12.9%	12.1%	15.2%	15.6%

Source: BIGinsight.com

Can you spare $20,000?

Home ownership and all that it entails (e.g., furniture, heating, lighting) is probably the largest expense a consumer will ever have in his or her lifetime. In many cases, it is also the largest asset. Until the recession hit some financial institutions would allow consumers to have as little as 5% down on a mortgage. The recession hit the economy and rules for obtaining funding changed. Most lending agencies now require a 20% down payment, a strong banking record, and a rock-solid work record in order to receive a mortgage.

Something happened along the way to make home debt exciting, popular, and characterized as risk free. Home equity loans became all the rage. A home equity loan is a second loan taken out on your home, typically at an interest rate higher than your mortgage interest rate. Credit cards maxed out? Take out a home equity loan. Want a vacation? Take out a home equity loan. Yearning to build on to the house? Take out a home equity loan. After all, the loan is often for thirty years, so you have plenty of time to pay it off. Do you want to know the best thing about a home equity loan? Spread the payments over thirty years and the amount due each month is small! It didn't seem to matter that consumers were paying interest on thirty year loans.

Okay, let's get back to reality. Home equity loans should be taken out judiciously and be paid back as rapidly as possible. The truth of the matter is, however, consumers began to use home equity loans as a personal piggy bank. Check out Figure 3.6. Between July 2007 and July 2011, the percent of all consumers using a home equity loan continues to increase. By July 2011, 19.8% had a home equity loan. Consumers use this money to fix up their homes, decrease credit card debt, take a vacation, and so on. Regardless of what they use the money for, they still need to pay it back—the money is not free. And as more consumers in this bracket are borrowing on their houses, it looks like a case of robbing Peter to pay Paul.

Now let's look at the percentage of consumers in households earning $75,000 or more that had a home equity loan. Earning a large salary did not make them immune from needing another source of income. These homes were so big that the mortgage industry called the loans "jumbo loans." Who cared if you needed a second mortgage because you didn't have enough money as a down payment? You were moving into your mini-castle. You now had really big bragging rights. The good news was that this group of consumers ($75,000+ households) learned its lesson about the negative state of the economy. Between July 2007 and July 2011, a downward trend was identified in consumers who obtained a second mortgage. In July 2007, 25.4% of consumers in this group had a second mortgage. By July 2011, this figure dropped to 17.3%. Before you say, "Oh sure, it is easy to stay within your budget when you make $75,000," think about all the *wealthy* people who go broke. Willie Nelson, Mike Tyson, Kim Basinger, Marvin Gaye, Jerry Lee Lewis, Burt Reynolds, MC Hammer, Gary Coleman, Judy Garland, and Michael Jackson all had money and let it slip away (From Riches to Rags, 2011). Anyone can lose their money and home if they are not watchful.

FIGURE 3.6: CONSUMERS WITH A HOME EQUITY LOAN

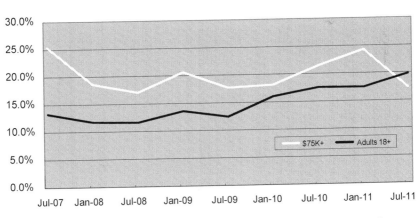

Source: BIGinsight.com

Big brother's help: Who wants it?

Foreclosures played a big role in the economic meltdown of the new millennium. Big houses, overextended credit, and ignoring the checking and savings account balance placed many homeowners in peril. It wasn't just the average citizen who couldn't pay the mortgage. Celebrities had their fair share of economic woes. Professional baseball players are known for big paychecks. Unfortunately for Lenny Dykstra, former New York Mets and Philadelphia Phillies centerfielder, the paychecks didn't cover the mortgage payments. He filed for bankruptcy in July 2009 and the bank foreclosed on his $18 million mansion (The Real Deal, 2009).

Foreclosures across the country are wreaking havoc on the economic stability of the housing market. In Tulsa, one out of 154 homes had a foreclosure filing during the first three months of 2010 (Evatt, 2010). States suffering from foreclosures the worst include Nevada, Arizona, California, Florida, and Michigan. The increase in foreclosures has resulted in a drop of home prices by more than 20% (Fifield & Rappeport, 2010).

President Obama announced a $1.5 billion support plan for the housing agencies to assist the worst hit states. Specifically, the plan would help residents of Nevada, Arizona, California, Florida, and Michigan who are facing foreclosure (Fifield & Rappeport, 2010). We decided to ask respondents over eighteen in an American Pulse™ Survey (N=4043) their opinions regarding the government's assistance. Specifically, consumers were asked three questions to measure their attitude toward the housing crisis and the foreclosures. Consumers expressed three very different opinions regarding government assistance with foreclosures.

The largest group consists of 45% of the consumers polled, as revealed in Figure 3.7, indicate that they believe that the U.S. government should help consumers with refinancing in order to avoid foreclosure. Whereas, 38.1% thought the U.S. government should not get involved.

People who default on their loans deserve to lose their homes. These two groups are at opposing sides. They also represent consumers across the nation since homeowners are trying to either maintain a solid property value or hold on to their house. A third group (16.4%) doesn't care what the government does.

Keeping up with the Jones's used to refer to buying as many possessions as your neighbors. Living the philosophy of keeping up with the Jones's may have driven many families down the road to bigger houses, more luxuries than they could afford, and directly into the cul-de-sac called foreclosure.

FIGURE 3.7: Consumers' Opinions Regarding Government Assistance

I don't think the U.S. government should get involved ... when people default on their loans, it is their own fault	38.1%
The U.S. government should allow people to refinance with government insurance if they are unable to pay adjustable rate mortgages to keep them out of foreclosure	45.5%
I don't care what the U.S. government does ... the "crisis" doesn't affect me	16.4%

Source: BIGinsight.com

Summary

Throughout history, parents worked hard and hoped, even dreamed, that their children would grow into successful adults. Today, many parents watch as their children's homes are foreclosed, downsized, or subsidized with multiple mortgages. The era of huge houses, living up to the neighbors' standards, and purchasing on credit are gone.

Consumers are faced with the harsh reality that the golden standard of living has changed.

Consumers are divided on how to fix the damaged housing market. Government assistance is wanted by some, while others want consumers to be responsible for their actions. One thing everyone agrees upon; it will take time for the housing market to recover.

Top five lessons learned

1. The American dream for a castle is turning into an albatross around the necks of many.

2. "Security first" are the watchwords when looking for a home loan. Consumers are obtaining a fixed loan in order to keep financial stability in their lives.

3. More single consumers are purchasing a home than in the past.

4. Home equity loans are equal opportunity sources of additional income. Consumers with incomes under $75,000 are increasingly obtaining a second mortgage.

5. Consumers are divided regarding the U.S. government's involvement in helping save the housing market.

References

Center for Disease Control and Prevention (2011). "Marriage and Divorce." Retrieved February 13, 2011 from http://www.cdc.gov/nchs/fastats/divorce.htm

Evatt, R. "Home Foreclosures Increase: The Tulsa Area Shows 29 Percent Boost from the Last Quarter of 2009 to the First Quarter of this Year." *Tulsa World* (April 15, 2010)

Fifield, A. and A. Rappeport. "U.S. Home Loan Foreclosures Reach Record High." *The Financial Times* (February 20, 2010) 3.

The Real Deal. "Stars Facing Home Foreclosures, Auctions." (July 10, 2009)

"From Riches to Rags: Ten Stars Who Went Broke." (2011) Accessed August 23, 2011 from http://www.cosmoloan.com/loans/from-riches-to-rags-10-celebrities-who-went-broke.html

Chapter

4

Consumers' Love Affair with Automobiles

The Big Three. Say those words and most people will know that you are talking about Chrysler, Ford, and General Motors (GM). The trio has been fierce rivals for decades—although the pool of competitors has grown significantly with globalization. The belief "buy American" hasn't applied to the automobile industry. Honda, Hyundai, Nissan, and Toyota have made significant inroads into the domestic market. And in the luxury market, BMW, Mercedes Benz, and Jaguar are cars for the consumers who want to drive in style.

Regardless of the make, model, or year of car you drive, consumers have a love affair with automobiles. Why else would so many people go annually to the car show at Cobo Hall in Detroit, Michigan? This chapter examines the need for power through our automobiles.

Cash for clunkers

When it comes to advertising, slogans that are simple and attract attention are often very successful. As you read the following slogans, what images come to mind?

- Just do it
- The ultimate driving machine
- It does a body good
- Snap, crackle, pop!
- The king of beers
- You'll never roam alone

Did you immediately think of the product? (Nike, BMW, Milk Board, Kellogg's Rice Krispies, Budweiser, and Travelocity.) Did the phrase bring back fond memories of using the product? Did you want a Budweiser beer or bowl of cereal? If so, the slogan was successful in marketing the product.

Effective slogans are designed to impel consumers into action. This brings us to "cash for clunkers"—officially known as the Car Allowance Rebate System (CARS). In 2009, the automobile industry suffered right along with the rest of the economy. At the beginning of the recession, consumers held back on the purchase of a new car. In an effort to stimulate auto sales, the government (President Obama) created CARS or cash for clunkers. The program was designed to (a) reduce the number of higher fuel automobiles on the road, (b) stimulate auto sales, and (c) provide buyers with up to a $4,500 rebate on the purchase of new cars (Carty, 2010).

The government originally allocated $1 billion for cash for clunkers. The enormous number of Americans that participated in the program prompted the government to provide an additional $2 billion to the program. Ultimately, 680,000 cars were sold under the program nationwide (Carty, 2010).

We asked consumers if the cash for clunkers program was the main reason they purchased a new car. Take a look at Figure 4.1. We separated the consumers into two groups: consumers living in households with an income of $50,000 or more and all those over the age of eighteen. Regardless of the group, less than 8% of consumers purchased a new car because of the cash for clunkers program.

Consumers in households earning $50,000 or more were more prone to participate in the program (7.5%) than consumers over the age of eighteen (6.1%). Reasons may have included increased discretionary income for a down payment or easier access for a car loan.

FIGURE 4.1: CASH FOR CLUNKERS PROGRAM

Was the "cash for clunkers" program a main reason for your purchase of a car?

	$50K+	Adults 18+
Yes	7.5%	6.1%
No	92.5%	93.9%

Source: BIGinsight.com

Purchase intentions

Anyone who has ever purchased a vehicle probably had two thoughts either right before or immediately after the purchase: (a) there is nothing like the aroma of a new car; and (b) the second a new car rolls off the lot its value drops by at least 25%.

Even though the value of a new car decreases substantially and rapidly, there are many reasons to purchase a new vehicle. Important additions such as side air bags or better crash safety records can prompt a purchase. Other consumers may want enhanced luxuries such as seat warmers, satellite radio capabilities, or a DVD system in the rear area for the children.

Between July 2004 and 2011, we asked consumers their purchase intentions regarding their next vehicle. We segmented the consumers into two groups: all consumers over the age of eighteen and those in households earning $75,000 or more.

Figure 4.2 shows us that in July 2004, 9.9% of all consumers intended to purchase a new vehicle. That same year, 13.0% of consumers with household incomes of $75,000 or more planned to purchase a vehicle. Then the economy tanked. The recession lingered on ... and on ... and on. National headlines called it Recession 2.0, the Great Recession, and the Lesser Depression. It didn't matter what consumers called it, between 2008 and 2011, the economy hit consumers and businesses hard. The automobile industry and its dealers responded by offering incentives and discounts. By July 2011, consumers were buying cars again: 12.1% of all adults planned to purchase a car; and 14.7% of consumers in $75,000 or higher income households planned to do the same. Dealer incentives and discounts worked.

FIGURE 4.2: VEHICLE PURCHASE INTENTIONS

| | Plan to Purchase a New Vehicle | | | | | | | |
	Jul-04	Jul-05	Jul-06	Jul-07	Jul-08	Jul-09	Jul-10	Jul-11
All	9.9%	9.3%	10.2%	12.2%	9.4%	10.0%	12.0%	12.1%
$75,000+	13.0%	11.3%	11.4%	14.9%	12.9%	12.2%	14.0%	14.7%

Source: BIGinsight.com

Attraction to vehicles

Henry Ford said, "Any customer can have a car painted any color that he wants so long as it is black." Times certainly have changed. Consumers are able to select color, style, design, textures, and level of friendliness to the environment. Automobiles come in a variety of shapes, sizes, and personalities.

For many consumers, the selection of a vehicle is associated with their personality. Most consumers keep an automobile anywhere from three to ten years. Some would say they keep their vehicles longer than they hold on to their spouses.

A vehicle needs to be reliable, like a best friend. It needs to be trustworthy; such that it can service the consumer's needs (such as carry the children, tote the lumber, and provide safety in an accident). As you can imagine, perceptions of the preferred automobile varies among individuals.

Between July 2004 and July 2011, we asked consumers about their automobile purchase intentions, in these automobile categories: (a) car, (b) truck, (c) minivan, (d) SUV, (e) crossover, and (f) hybrid.

Let's address the issue of automobiles based on classification. Take a look at Figure 4.2. In July 2004, cars were the most desired vehicle by men (63.1%) and women (61.1%). Next, we asked about the ever-popular truck. The truck has long been touted as a "real man's" vehicle. Before SUVs, the truck was the vehicle that separated the men from the boys. The data revealed, however, that, in July 2004, 14.5% of women were also attracted to this multi-purpose vehicle—compared with 21.6% of men. By July 2008, the recession was in full swing and the percentage of consumers seeking to purchase a truck had dropped—just like the economy. Only 14.3% of men and 10.3% of women were considering this type of vehicle. Their decisions could have been a combination of the economy and the wider variety of vehicle styles available (for example, the crossover). July 2011 looked better for truck dealers as men's interest in trucks grew slightly to 20.3%. Only a small percentage of women came back to the truck market. With 11.3% of women considering a truck, I suspect the various SUVs and crossover vehicles proved to be more attractive to this group.

The minivan is known as the vehicle of choice for the soccer mom. Minivans became a popular alternative to the car because of size. They hold more people and equipment than a car yet were easy to drive. In July 2004, the minivan proved popular with men (11.4%) and women (19.2%). By July 2011, however, only 8.5% of men and 10.5% of women considered purchasing a minivan. This dramatic drop in popularity was due primarily to the many different rival vehicle offerings, namely, the SUV and the crossover.

The sport utility vehicle—or SUV—became the darling of the automotive industry. It was more compact than the minivan, but was "sexier" and less of a "mom-mobile." The SUV was designed to be attractive to both genders and used for any and all types of purposes. In other words, this vehicle was meant to be sold to the masses. Automobile dealers could see dollar signs from miles away as consumers readily accepted the SUV.

In July 2004, 28.3% of men and 21.8% of women surveyed considered purchasing an SUV. Throughout the period surveyed, the percent of men intending to purchase an SUV declined, reaching 19.9% in July 2011. Over the same time, the percent of women driving an SUV increased to 24.2%. Clearly this vehicle brought joy to the automobile industry.

Now let's look at the crossover. The crossover possesses attributes of more than one vehicle. For example, a vehicle that includes all-wheel drive and a four-wheel independent suspension, tire pressure monitoring system, and V6 engine would be considered a crossover. In July 2004, 9.1% of men and 9.2% of women intended to purchase a crossover vehicle. By July 2011, men intending to purchase this type of vehicle increased to 10%. During this same time period, women showed a marked increase in interest in this vehicle. In July 2011, 17.7% of the women surveyed indicated an intention to purchase a crossover. The automobile industry had another design darling on its hands.

Now to discuss the car seen as green, or friendly to the environment, and frequently adopted by Hollywood stars—the hybrid. The hybrid car offers consumers a balance between gasoline and electricity. The vehicle is more expensive to the consumer, provides a higher markup for the dealer, and is targeted toward a specific group of consumers, those who are concerned about the environment.

In July 2005, we surveyed consumers' intentions to purchase a hybrid vehicle. We found that 11.8% of men and 9.9% of women considered purchasing a hybrid. By 2011, men's interest in purchasing a hybrid decreased to 7.9%. Women's intentions decreased as well—6.3% planned to buy a hybrid during July 2011.

FIGURE 4.2: TYPE OF AUTOMOTIVE PURCHASE CONSIDERATIONS

	Jul-04	Jul-05	Jul-06	Jul-07	Jul-08	Jul-09	Jul-10	Jul-11
Car								
Men	63.1%	63.7%	65.8%	65.2%	62.0%	58.0%	59.3%	60.1%
Women	61.1%	59.9%	63.2%	58.3%	62.2%	63.8%	51.8%	61.9%
Truck								
Men	21.6%	17.3%	18.6%	15.3%	14.3%	23.7%	19.4%	20.3%
Women	14.5%	16.9%	16.4%	14.3%	10.3%	11.3%	11.6%	11.3%
Minivan								
Men	11.4%	15.1%	9.5%	9.4%	8.6%	10.1%	7.8%	8.5%
Women	19.2%	16.7%	14.2%	13.8%	6.4%	9.0%	11.6%	10.5%
SUV								
Men	28.3%	23.3%	21.4%	24.7%	15.8%	19.8%	18.9%	19.9%
Women	21.8%	23.4%	23.6%	20.4%	22.9%	27.5%	29.3%	24.2%
Crossover								
Men	9.1%	8.1%	7.3%	8.5%	15.7%	13.9%	12.0%	10.0%
Women	9.2%	13.8%	13.5%	18.2%	16.5%	18.0%	14.9%	17.7%
Hybrid								
Men		11.8%	9.4%	12.6%	16.1%	13.3%	9.3%	7.9%
Women		9.9%	10.3%	11.4%	13.4%	12.5%	7.4%	6.3%

Source: BIGinsight.com

What's hot, what's not

Paris Hilton might have made the expression "that's hot" famous, but it was consumers who made the Ford Motor Company hot and profitable. Okay, maybe Ford CEO Alan Mulally had a little something to do with it. He brought back the popular Taurus, straightened out the finances, and discontinued unprofitable models. Ford was also the only car company not to go (in a private plane and chauffeured car) groveling to Capitol Hill for bailout money.

In March 2010, we asked consumers to give their opinions regarding seven different car companies. Specifically, we asked which company brands were hot, and which were not. We segmented consumers into two groups: consumers in households earning $50,000 or more; and all consumers over the age of eighteen. The companies examined included Chrysler, Ford, GM, Honda, Hyundai, Nissan, and Toyota.

Consumers in households earning $50,000 or more voiced their opinions loud and clear regarding automobile brand preferences. Figure 4.3 reveals that the "hottest" car manufacturer was the Ford Motor Company with 66.5% of the group. Meanwhile, Honda came in a strong second with 58.2%.

In the beginning of this chapter, we spoke about the Big Three—Chrysler, Ford, and GM. Based on opinions of consumers in households earning $50,000 or more, perhaps we should redefine the Big Three. Originally, it referred to the automobile manufacturers based in the state of Michigan. Yet, GM was considered hot by only 37.4% of consumers in $50,000 or higher households, and only 21.2% thought Chrysler was hot. The imported brands were far more popular, and considered "hotter", than GM and Chrysler: Honda (58.2%), Hyundai (45.2%), and Nissan (44.5%).

However, it's hard to avoid noticing the higher-earning consumers' opinions of one of these imported brands—Toyota. Only 19% of this group thought this company was hot. This survey was taken when the company experienced a widespread flaw in the acceleration system.

Thousands of cars were recalled. Akio Toyoda, president and CEO of the company, was called before Congress to discuss the numerous problems that plagued the company.

Part of Ford's success with consumers could be its actions. For the first time in the company's history, they had a CEO (Alan Mulally) whose last name wasn't Ford. This earth-shattering move told consumers that the Ford family cared more about the company then their egos. More action followed. The Taurus was brought back. For years, the Taurus was one of the most popular cars in the country. Ford had retired the car. The new CEO brought it back. Consumers rejoiced. They loved the Taurus. This action said, "We made a mistake and we will correct it."

Other designs were phased out. The company focused on its stronger models. New ones were introduced. This company was moving forward—fast, just like its engines.

Now look at all consumers aged eighteen and older. Their opinions mirrored those of consumers in the $50,000 and higher households. The Ford Motor Company was considered the "hottest" company (66%), again followed by Honda (57.6%). With the exception of Toyota, the other foreign companies under consideration beat out GM and Chrysler. Toyota? Well, let's just say the company has had better days—only 22% of this group thought it was hot.

FIGURE 4.3: HOT SELLING VEHICLES

| | $50,000+ | | All Consumers | |
	Hot	Not	Hot	Not
Chrysler	21.2%	78.8%	26.1%	73.9%
Ford	66.5%	33.5%	66.0%	34.0%
GM	37.4%	62.6%	41.6%	58.4%
Honda	58.2%	41.8%	57.6%	42.4%
Hyundai	45.2%	54.8%	44.4%	55.6%
Nissan	44.5%	55.5%	46.2%	53.8%
Toyota	19.0%	81.0%	22.0%	78.0%

Source: BIGinsight.com

Slow down, you move too fast

Let's talk about Toyota and its problems—everyone else has, but we are in a position to give a unique perspective on how it has had an impact on consumers' perceptions. Cars are designed to go fast—very fast. Get on an interstate and some drivers will accelerate to in excess of 80 miles an hour regardless of the speed limit. Of course, they can always slow down when needed—when traffic gets heavy or when approaching a police car.

In late 2009, drivers of Toyota model cars experienced a new sensation. Some of the cars accelerated without the assistance of the driver. These runaway cars were linked to eight different models sold throughout the U.S. and worldwide (Rechtin, 2010). Toyota was concerned for consumers' safety, naturally, but it also had an advertising and media nightmare on its hands.

Two possible causes for the unintended acceleration were identified: sticky throttle pedals and incorrectly installed floor mats (Rechtin, 2010). Regardless of the reason, millions of consumers began to look at Toyota as an unsafe car manufacturer. Toyota issued a recall on eight models. Between November 2009 and September 2010, 10.5 million Toyota vehicles were recalled throughout the U.S. An additional 2.5 million vehicles were recalled worldwide (Rechtin, 2010).

There is a saying in advertising that "perception is oftentimes reality." What really matters is what the consumers perceive to be real. If this is true, Toyota's problems extend further than the eight models that were deemed unsafe. Word-of-mouth promotion from friends and relatives, positive advertising, and a sleek new design or features (for example, heated seats) are incentives for consumers to switch automobile brands. However, safety concerns will often override any new feature, exterior color, or recommendation by a celebrity.

Take a look at Figure 4.4. In March 2010, we asked consumers if the Toyota recall made them consider other brands. We separated the consumers into two groups: consumers living in households with an income of $50,000 or more; and all consumers over the age of eighteen.

Of the consumers in households with $50,000 or higher income, 34.4% believed the Toyota recall made them consider a different brand as their first or second automobile choice. The percentage of all consumers was higher: 40.2% said they considered other brands as a result of the recall.

FIGURE 4.4: TOYOTA RECALL INFLUENCED DECISION TO SEEK A DIFFERENT BRAND

	$50,000+	All Consumers
Yes	34.4%	40.2%
No	65.6%	59.8%

Source: BIGinsight.com

Congress has its say

Just when Toyota was trying to manage consumers' concerns over safety, Congress "invited" the CEO to speak about the issues at hand. Cable, national, and local news stations covered the hearings. Consumers nationwide watched via television and streaming video as the CEO of Toyota, Mr. Toyoda, apologized about the safety issues. His humility, apologies, and grief were evident. No one watching the hearings could deny that Mr. Toyoda wanted to be anywhere but in Washington. He obviously wished he could turn back the hands of time and fix the problems.

In March 2010, we asked consumers if the recalls and the congressional hearings hurt the Toyota brand. We separated the consumers into two groups: consumers living in households with an income of $50,000 or more; and all consumers over the age of eighteen.

Regardless of income, Figure 4.5 shows that over 80% of consumers said the recall and hearings hurt the brand. Talk about a firestorm. Branding is critical to the success of any company. Building a successful brand takes years, sometimes decades. Some companies are never able to completely build a sturdy brand. For Toyota, one problem—albeit a widespread and significant problem—created a chain reaction, which resulted in the recall. The recall resulted in a congressional hearing. The congressional hearing resulted in widespread negative publicity. Widespread negative publicity resulted in consumers' lack of belief in the brand. Between January and September 2010, Toyota was the only major automotive company with a decline in sales (Rechtin, 2010). Perceptions and branding matter!

FIGURE 4.5: CONGRESSIONAL HEARINGS ON TOYOTA HURT THE COMPANY

	$50,000+	All Consumers
Yes	83.1%	80.4%
No	16.9%	19.6%

Source: BIGinsight.com

Summary

A vehicle has traditionally been a visible symbol of a person's character. The color, style, brand, and personality of the car represented the actual or desired image of the consumer. The automobile industry has had its fair share of ups and downs. However, during one of the worst economic times since the Great Depression of the 1930s, one company proved that going back to the basics can bring loyal consumers, sales, and profits. The Ford Motor Company did the unthinkable and hired a CEO who didn't have the name "Ford." GM and Chrysler asked for (and received) help from the government. Toyota kept Congress busy with inquiries regarding safety. What is certain is that, during all the economic woes, the automobile industry added "flavor" to the daily news.

Top five lessons learned

1. Just because an industry is in the private sector doesn't mean the government won't get involved. The cash for clunkers program and the Toyota recall demonstrates the polar ends of the government's outreach to the automobile industry.

2. Vehicle preferences are changing rapidly. The once popular minivan is being replaced by other vehicles.

3. Vehicles possess definite personalities, and they are marketed toward specific genders and groups.

4. An SUV is popular by men and women.

5. The Congressional Hearings on the Toyota recall hurt the company as perceived by the consumer.

References

Carty, S. S. "Clunkers Program Worked for a While." *USA Today* (August 31, 2010) 4B.

Rechtin, M. "Toyota Will Push Safety in Ad Blitz." *Automotive News* Vol. 85 (September 6, 2010) 1.

Wilson, A. "Sales Stink, but Smell Those Sweet Profits." *Automotive News* Vol. 85 (September 6, 2010) 1.

Chapter

5

Let the Retailer Beware: Consumers Are in the Driver's Seat

The shopping experience has changed dramatically as a result of technology. The store was once either a general store—anyone remember Woolworth's?—or a traditional department store. A department store, a real department store, carried every category of merchandise including furniture. The department store opened a world of opportunities to the consumer. This form of retailing had a long and strong run. Technology changed the world including how consumers shopped. Imported products, higher quality products, and online retailing influenced consumers' purchase decisions. Instead of being satisfied with local products, they searched online for unique items. Instead of automatically shopping at department stores, consumers sought out specialty and discount stores. Retailers started to consider what consumers wanted, how they shopped, and why they shopped. Consumers, not the retailers, now dictated much of the retail industry.

15% off everything in the store

Coupons were very popular during the '60s and '70s. Direct mail helped increase the popularity of coupons. Consumers clipped coupons out of newspapers and magazines to save anywhere from 25 cents to $1 on groceries or school supplies. It was considered frugal and part of the household budget process. Clipping coupons took time and required some organization skills. Consumers needed to be aware of brands, expiration dates, and size requirements. The recession in the new millennium brought resurgence in the popularity of coupons and saving money.

Rising gas prices were on most consumers' minds between 2006 and 2011. A country long devoted to vehicles was faced with fluctuating gas prices. The popular SUV and trucks ate up gas at an alarming rate. As consumers pumped gas in their tanks, their wallets felt the pinch.

In July 2006, we asked consumers if they used coupons more as a result of fluctuating gas prices. As you see in Figure 5.1, 22.6% of all households and 17.6% of households earning $75,000+ used coupons more. The trend for using coupons continued to increase. By July 2011, 38.8% of all households and 35.5% of households earning $75,000 used coupons. Coupons have become a mainstay of one-third of households nationwide, regardless of income. Coupon clippers were united in the effort to save money.

Manufacturers and retailers are becoming far shrewder regarding the distribution of coupons. An integrated distribution is often used. Coupons are located on websites, sent to e-mail addresses, in newspapers, magazines, and direct mail. These coupons provide consumers with a percentage or dollar amount off the selling price—a price typically already discounted. Today's consumer is indeed becoming very price sensitive and shopping savvy. Gas prices continue to fluctuate but at least the savings from coupons can act as a partial reprieve from the sticker shock at the pump.

FIGURE 5.1: Using Coupons More as a Result of Fluctuating Gas Prices

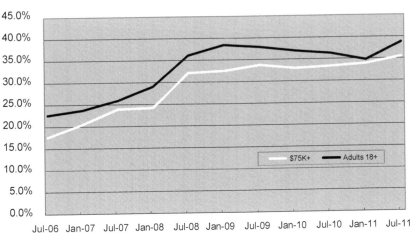

Source: BIGinsight.com

Closeout sale!

When the recession hit, the popularity of shopping at the mall came to a grinding halt. It was no longer fun to window shop. People didn't have money for luxuries and the temptation to pick up "a little something" was squashed. With the exodus of consumers from the malls, retailers had an abundance of inventory and debt. They needed to attract consumers into the stores and entice them into purchasing. It wasn't going to be easy. Consumers were nervous over the continuing state of the recession; layoffs were reported daily in the newspapers, and uncertainty reigned across America. The consumers' love affair with SUVs and large cars didn't help matters. Gas guzzlers ate an increasing amount of the family's limited budget as oil prices rose.

After 9/11, the economy turned upside down. Nothing seemed to work the same. For some retailers, the bottom had dropped out of the market. Branch locations were closed; or simply shutting their doors altogether.

Retailers were required to take a strong stance in order to draw consumers into the store. They resorted to the dreaded four-letter word—but this time, the retailers meant it—*Sale!* Whenever a retailer placed merchandise on sale, really on sale, they priced the merchandise at a lower markup than usual. This resulted in a lower profit for the retailer. On the bright side, if the product sold, the retailer moved the goods and made room for new inventory.

Take a look at Figure 5.2. In July 2006, 32.5% of all consumers and 26.7% of consumers earning $75,000 or more shopped for sale items more often. By July 2011, the percent of consumers seeking sales had increased to 42.2% and 39.5% respectively. For consumers, this meant that an increasing number of consumers looked for a good deal.

FIGURE 5.2: SHOPPING FOR SALES MORE OFTEN AS A RESULT OF FLUCTUATING GAS PRICES

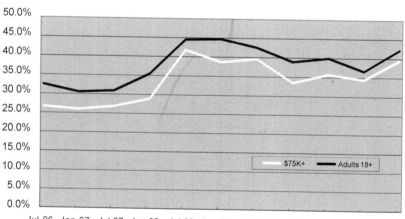

Source: BIGinsight.com

As the trend for shopping for sale items increased, it meant that retailers were stuck offering sale merchandise. After all, one of the most difficult acts in retailing is to raise prices once they have been lowered. Consumers get angry when they have to pay higher prices.

They can become fickle and take their business elsewhere. We can expect the lower prices and big signs indicating "Sale" to be a trend that will continue for a very long time—especially since recovery in the economy is nowhere in sight.

Is this the real deal?

During the 1970s, generic food brands hit the market. The products were low quality and very cheap—not just inexpensive, we are talking cheap! We use the word "cheap" on purpose. Consumers could purchase a can of peas for 15 cents. The can was wrapped in white paper with black letters that said *PEAS*.

Now it's a new millennium; we are in a recession, and it is once more a good time to save money. A wide variety of retailers have adopted generic or store brand merchandise to offer to the thrifty consumer. Target, Walmart, Nordstrom, Walgreens, and Kroger are examples of stores that have developed successful generic brands. These brands accomplish two goals for the retailer. One, they bring the consumer into that particular store, thereby, building loyalty. Two, they have higher profit margins.

In July 2006, we surveyed consumers' purchasing patterns of store and generic brands as a result of fluctuating gas prices. Figure 5.3 reveals that 22.6% of all households and 12.6% of households earning $75,000 or more purchased store or generic brands. By July 2011, acceptance of store and generic brands jumped to 35.5% and 26.5% respectively.

Part of the acceptance of store and generic brands can be attributed to the lack of confidence in the economy. Economic times have continued to badly affect the consumer household discretionary income. Consumers have cut back on spending, and generic and store brands were an easy method of saving money. However, we need to give credit where credit is due. Retailers have become increasingly more aggressive in reaching out to meet consumers' needs. In a recession, retailers have reacted by developing higher quality store brands than offered in the past. The store brands are priced significantly lower than national brands, yet compete in style and offering. Once upon a time, store brands were placed in secondary locations; national brands were given premier locations throughout the store. Today store brands adoption by consumers has earned the right to prime placement and visibility throughout the store. Store brands have been heavily marketed in advertising campaigns. Consumers have responded in turn by purchasing the store brands and saving on the bottom line.

FIGURE 5.3: GENERIC BRAND PURCHASE PATTERNS AS A RESULT OF FLUCTUATING GAS PRICES

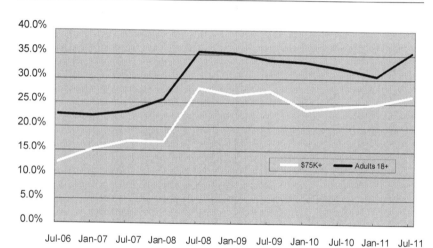

Source: BIGinsight.com

The pied piper of consumers

As consumers of all income brackets have come to accept store brand goods, there has been a similar process in terms of retailers. During the '60s and '70s, Kmart was the most successful retailer in America as defined by sales and profits. This company truly knew how to bring in the mass market, but this did not include the upper classes. Kmart was clearly for the lower and middle class—for the people who needed to save money. Consumers ran when they saw the blue light flashing. They knew this meant extra savings. People who earned $75,000 or more shopped at Saks Fifth Avenue, Lord & Taylor, or Neiman Marcus. Everyone else bought their clothes at Kmart during the blue light specials.

During the late 1990s, Kohl's strength as a retailer grew. The retailer classified itself as a department store. Consumers of all income brackets flocked to the hip retailer. Our survey of consumers revealed that in July 2002, 4.3% of females and 5.4% of females in households earning $75,000 or more shopped at Kohl's. By July 2011, these figures jumped to 13.4% and 18.2% respectively. This meant that females of all household incomes shop at Kohl's.

Before we analyze the reason behind Kohl's success, let's look at the men. Figure 5.4 revealed that in July 2002, 2.4% of all men and 3.1% of men in households earning $75,000 or more shopped at Kohl's for women's clothing. By July 2011, their patronage jumped to 7.9% and 14.4% respectively.

FIGURE 5.4: SHOP AT KOHL'S MOST OFTEN FOR WOMEN'S CLOTHING

	Jul-02	Jul-03	Jul-04	Jul-05	Jul-06	Jul-07	Jul-08	Jul-09	Jul-10	Jul-11
All males	2.4%	3.1%	3.1%	4.5%	5.2%	6.5%	6.5%	7.2%	7.3%	7.9%
All females	4.3%	4.6%	6.2%	6.6%	8.2%	9.4%	10.4%	11.4%	12.6%	13.4%
$75K+ males	3.1%	5.8%	7.4%	7.7%	7.7%	10.8%	9.8%	11.2%	11.7%	14.4%
$75K+ females	5.4%	9.3%	10.9%	12.1%	14.6%	12.0%	12.8%	14.9%	18.0%	18.2%

Source: BIGinsight.com

Kohl's found the secret to retail success in the new millennium. The retailer brought in designer brand names known to households in the $75,000 range. Dana Buchman and Vera Wang designs were revised for the company and its consumers. Brand name kitchen items brought in foodies who loved to have a stocked kitchen—even if they didn't cook. Sale prices every week kept the consumer traffic coming through the doors. Kohl's distributed coupons by the thousands; consumers received 15% off everything—yes, everything—in the store. Consumers responded with loyal patronage to the company.

Need a parking space at the mall?

In real estate, the three most important criteria have always been location, location, and location. For retailers, perhaps the three most important criteria have always been consumer traffic, consumer traffic, and consumer traffic. There is a lot of anecdotal evidence about retailing, which has been passed down from retailer to retailer. For example:

- It takes ten people to walk by a store before one consumer walks into it.

- One out of every five consumers walks by a store window and does not even know that the store exists.

- Shopping malls served as a "baby-sitter" for teenagers during the '90s. Consumers often eat at the food court before going into a store.

- Teenagers spend more money at the food court than any other store in a mall.

- Consumers spend more money when purchasing with a credit card.

The above may just be stories passed down by retailers, but they come across as very real. Think about it, how many times have you walked through a mall and said, "I don't recall ever seeing that store before?" Or passed through the food court and thought, "Wow, there isn't one empty table, doesn't anyone eat at home?" And maybe you upsized the gift to your spouse when you pulled out your Visa card?

During the '80s, malls were crowded and it was difficult to find a parking spot. Back in the '90s, shopping at the mall was comparable to armed warfare. First, you needed to go early to find a parking space. If you were lucky, you found a space that wasn't in the tow-away zone or a mile from the department store door. You braced yourself to battle the wall-to-wall crowds. Ah, the smell of victory when you edged yourself in between the crowds and the racks. The excitement of the mall gave you a thrill. The consumer battle cry was "Charge it!"

Then the world changed, with 9/11 and the recession. America changed and so did consumers' attitudes and actions. As fast as the malls had once filled, they emptied. Retailers found themselves staring at racks of inventory and not enough consumer traffic. Check out Figure 5.5. In July 2006, 47.3% of all females and 44.8% of females in households earning $75,000 or more took fewer shopping trips. Consumer caution on shopping continued. By July 2011, the percentage had increased to 50.0% for all females and 46.6% for females in households earning $75,000 or more.

FIGURE 5.5: TAKING FEWER SHOPPING TRIPS AS A RESULT OF FLUCTUATING GAS PRICES

	Jul-06	Jul-07	Jul-08	Jul-09	Jul-10	Jul-11
All males 18+	36.7%	34.4%	45.5%	38.5%	33.1%	38.4%
All females 18+	47.3%	44.7%	58.6%	47.5%	43.9%	50.0%
$75K+ males	35.9%	33.0%	47.4%	38.4%	33.1%	36.2%
$75K+ females	44.8%	45.7%	59.0%	47.1%	39.8%	46.6%

Source: BIGinsight.com

It wasn't only females who changed their shopping habit. Figure 5.5 reveals that men also stayed away from retailers. In July 2006, 36.7%

of all men and 35.9% of men in households earning $75,000 or more took fewer shopping trips. The percentages increased slightly by July 2011 to 38.4% and 36.2% respectively. Shopping meant spending money—money that consumers needed for bills and unexpected expenses in the future.

Wired

We've learned that consumer purchasing patterns changed during the new millennium. Consumers became more price-conscious as well as more cautious about wasting gas to run all over town to different stores and malls. Discount stores offered more fashion-forward merchandise for price-sensitive consumers, regardless of the household income. So how are consumers acquiring products?

In January 2011, the *Wall Street Journal* reported that online sales were at an all-time high of 15.4%. Consumers shopped from the comfort of their homes, the office, and Internet cafés. Anywhere a broadband signal was found; consumers logged on to the Internet and satisfied the need to purchase. A January 2011 survey of consumers revealed that men and women are shopping more via the Internet. Check out Figure 5.6.

Over the next ninety days, 21.8% of men planned to purchase more items through the Internet, while 13.7% of women planned to do the same. Convenience, access to a broader and deeper variety of merchandise, and national brands may be the impetus to buy online.

FIGURE 5.6: INTERNET SHOPPING PLANS OVER THE NEXT 90 DAYS

	Men	Women
More	21.8%	13.7%
Same	52.8%	52.0%
Less	25.4%	34.2%

Source: BIGinsight.com

Summary

Robert C. Gallagher said, "Change is inevitable—except from a vending machine." Consumers changing attitudes and behaviors toward the retail market were immediate, dramatic, and probably long term. When the recession hit and gas prices increased, consumers responded accordingly. They looked in their pockets and said, "No, I won't purchase until you give me a better deal."

Retailers in turn learned to listen to consumers' needs and wants. Discount retailers adopted fashionable products, and their stores slowly evolved into department-like retail operations. Store brand merchandise at lower than national brand prices offered consumers options. Online retailing further expanded consumers' world of product and service offerings. Men stepped up to the computer and started shopping online, thereby, avoiding malls and specialty stores. Retailers and consumers have learned to work together to satisfy a common goal: offer the right products and services at the right price.

Top five lessons learned

1. Coupons are extremely popular and highly desired by consumers. Coupons build traffic, generate sales, and build store loyalty.

2. Consumers are purchasing increasingly more store brands in combination with national brands. Successful store brand merchandise is carried by Target, Kohl's, and JCPenney.

3. Fashion-oriented discount stores are attracting consumers in all household income brackets. Fashions by top designers at popular prices are bringing consumers into Kohl's.

4. The popularity of malls continues to decline. They are no longer the designated "hang out" for shoppers and teens. As gas prices increase, the number of trips to the mall decreases.

5. Men are becoming increasingly more active online shoppers.

References

Zimmerman, A. "Gift Shoppers Flocked to the Web." *Wall Street Journal* (December 24, 2010) B1.

Chapter

6

Make Mine Large

You might call it chow, dinner, supper, or snack time, but regardless of how you designate it, "What's for dinner?" remains a favorite inquiry. As I observed in the previous chapter, you only have to walk by the food court next time you are in a mall and then look at the shopping lanes. Nine times out of ten, the food court will be busier. It is as if consumers believe they can't enter a mall without getting food.

It is no secret that the demographics and psychographics across the U.S. landscape have changed dramatically over the decade. One interesting trend has been the beautification of the kitchen. Stainless steel appliances, granite counter tops, and wood floors were in high demand regardless of the neighborhood, cost of the house, or the amount of actual use of the kitchen. Who cared if anyone in the house cooked? What mattered was that the kitchen looked as if a gourmet chef lived in the house.

Another trend is weight increase. According to the Centers for Disease Control and Prevention, 34% of adults twenty years and older are obese, with 68% of consumers classified as overweight (IBTimes, 2011).

Putting the two trends together, if consumers aren't cooking at home, they have to be getting their meals somewhere, and those meals are not as healthy as they could be. So the question that is begging to be answered is "Where (and what) do consumers eat?"

The answer to the question is fast-food restaurants (and, of course, fast food). Ray Kroc, the founder of McDonald's, was brilliant. Not just brilliant, he revolutionized the way food was delivered to the consumer. Fast, inexpensive, and easy to handle—what more could the consumer want? Consumers aren't discriminating about the nutritional value of their meal selections if the financial success of the fast-food industry is any gauge. McDonald's cash registers ring continuously worldwide—the company brings in excess of $13 billion in revenue annually (McDonald's Financial History, 2009). That's a lot of burgers and fries. Yum! Brands is nipping close behind McDonald's for customers. Yum! Brands includes KFC, Pizza Hut, and Taco Bell and has generated $10.8 billion in revenues during 2009 (2009 Yum! Brands Financial Highlights). You get the picture. Fast food, whether served through a window, at a counter, or a booth is big financial business. The term "super-size-me" refers to (a) the consumer's serving, (b) the eventual waistline and weight gain, and (c) the revenues generated by the company.

Throughout this chapter, the regular fast-food eaters will be examined. These restaurant gourmands are defined as consumers who dine at fast-food restaurants four or more times a week. You may think who could possibly eat at a fast-food restaurant four or more times a week? Well, millions of Americans dine in their car, drive through, or sit and read the paper while munching on fries every day of the week. Eating at fast-food restaurants is as normal to many consumers as breathing in air.

Men versus Women

Society often compares men and women. Which sex is stronger, smarter, healthier, richer and ad infinitum? Select a category and there probably has been a comparison based on sex. A popular comparison between the sexes is their eating patterns; specifically how much each gender ate out. We looked at the truth of this view. In May 2005, more men (55.4%) regularly ate (meaning four times a week) at fast-food restaurants than women (47.4%) in our survey (Figure 6.1). By May 2011, the numbers dropped; 41.3% of men continued to frequently get their meals in a box or bag, or on a plastic tray. These figure compared to 33.2% of women who were regular fast food eaters.

The next time you walk through a parking lot, casually glance inside the cars. Count the number of cars that have fast-food wrappers or empty soda bottles abandoned in the back seat. It is amazing the number of people that use the back seat of their car as a fast-food wastebasket. This is one battle that neither side wins.

FIGURE 6.1: MEN VS. WOMEN: REGULAR FAST FOOD EATERS

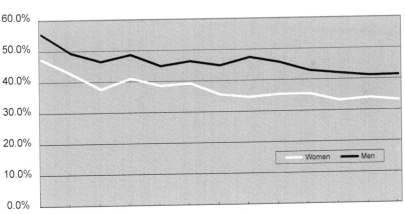

Source: BIGinsight.com

Who has time to cook?

Baby boomers were brought up on a new invention called TV dinners, while watching three channels on a thirteen-inch screen TV. One of the best television shows was called *Leave It to Beaver*. Mrs. Cleaver—the Beaver's mom—was always cooking or cleaning in high heels and pearls. Life was perfect for the Beaver and his family. Meals included meat, potatoes, milk, and a variety of deserts. Wally—Mr. Cleaver—married the perfect woman. Everyone wanted to live in the Cleaver family, or at least have a family life similar to theirs.

Then consumers woke up and smelled the coffee. The Cleaver family was entirely fictional! Fast-food restaurants came on the American landscape and attitudes about how married couples ate changed dramatically. They no longer had time to leisurely sit down at the dinner table for a big meal. Forget the gracious living through home-cooked meals. If Martha Stewart or Paula Dean wants to cook up a meal, welcome them into your home and give them a spatula. Otherwise, the majority of married couples are either too tired, too busy, or just don't want to cook. They exchange quality and refinement for ease and convenience.

Now look at Figure 6.2. Between May 2006 and May 2011, at least a third of married consumers ate four or more times a week at fast-food restaurants (dropping from half of married couples in 2005). At this rate, they hardly needed kitchens in their houses. A microwave and a mini refrigerator would suffice. The statistics provide us with a sense that fast food is a popular food source option for married couples.

The percent of singles who regularly ate at fast-food restaurants was higher than that of married couples. In May 2005, 54% ate four or more times a week at fast-food restaurants. By May 2011, this figure decreased to 42.2%. Perhaps the advertisements against fried foods were working. The statistics also reveal that those who were divorced were generally less likely to regularly eat out than either married couples or singles.

FIGURE 6.2: REGULAR FAST FOOD PATRONS BY MARITAL STATUS

	May-05	May-06	May-07	May-08	May-09	May-10	May-11
Married	50.4%	39.6%	38.6%	36.9%	39.0%	35.6%	36.1%
Single	54.0%	45.0%	47.1%	50.0%	47.4%	44.2%	42.2%
Divorced	50.7%	39.7%	36.6%	33.4%	32.1%	31.5%	30.8%

Source: BIGinsight.com

Land that I love

The South often gets beaten up in the press for the unhealthy lifestyle of its consumers. Southern-fried chicken, deep-fried turkey, and shrimp and grits are just some of the wonderful tastes of the South. Grease really is a staple of the cooking process, but, for example, at the popular South Carolina Lizard's Thicket restaurants, the result is delicious food—even if it is deep fried and could result in the customer packing on a few pounds. But enough talk of the South—which I dearly love.

According to our survey, Southerners certainly enjoyed the hospitality offered by fast-food restaurants (Figure 6.3). Between May 2005 and 2011, people who lived in the South were generally most likely to regularly eat at this type of establishment. Their patronage exceeded that of consumers elsewhere throughout the land. Whereas, the Northeast represented the smallest group of regular fast-food patrons, from 40.4% in May 2005 down to just 28.3% in May 2011.

FIGURE 6.3: REGULAR FAST FOOD PATRONS BY REGION

	May-05	May-06	May-07	May-08	May-09	May-10	May-11
Midwest	54.3%	43.8%	42.4%	41.6%	43.5%	37.4%	36.8%
Northeast	40.4%	30.7%	30.4%	30.5%	27.8%	31.6%	28.3%
South	54.3%	46.9%	46.6%	43.6%	45.0%	41.2%	42.3%
West	52.2%	41.9%	44.2%	42.1%	40.3%	37.8%	37.6%

Source: BIGinsight.com

The golden years

Some of my fondest memories are having Sunday dinner at my grandparents' house. Thinking back, I'm not sure if the meals served could be considered gourmet, but they always tasted great. Grilled cheese sandwiches, fried bologna sandwiches, pork chops with mashed potatoes and gravy, or tapioca pudding remind me of my grandparents and a sense of feeling loved. The menus served were probably as equally offensive to the American Heart Association as those served by the fast-food industry. The difference was the meals were made by family members. Does that matter? It did to me. Of course, when I was a child the fast-food industry was also in its infancy.

Now, in the twenty-first century, the older generation is referred to as the "gray market." It is characterized as traditional, willing to shop to find good bargains, and having a higher level of discretionary income than other age brackets (Dunne & Lusch, 2007). It is well documented that preparing meals at home is far more economical than eating out. Given the saving disposition of the gray market, it is logical to assume that older consumers would avoid patronizing fast-food restaurants. However, consumers don't always act rationally. It is also very unwise to assume anything—it can make a person (or company) look foolish.

Figure 6.4 reveals that in August 2007, 33.2% of the grandparents surveyed stated that they ate at fast-food restaurants four or more times a month. By August 2011, this figure declined to 30.4%. A little over one fourth of the elderly population surveyed regularly ate at fast-food restaurants. This is the generation that was brought up on healthy eating and learned how to cook. This is the Ozzie and Harriet generation. Is it the convenience? Perhaps it is the camaraderie of other consumers?

At first blush, you may think that this group is not important to the fast-food industry. Think again. Let's consider the grandparents' habits. Early-bird meal specials were made popular by their adoption by the gray market. This group wants to eat early and get home.

Likewise, grandparents often take care of their grandchildren during the day. Grandparents comprise an excellent sub-target market for fast-food restaurants. They patronize the restaurant when it is typically slow. They take the grandchildren there for a snack or meal. Any and all fast-food restaurants gleefully encourage the gray market and its money. But there remain some $50 million-dollar questions:

1. Will this target group continue to decline in patronage? Even a small decline will result in large financial losses.

2. Where is the group going to eat if not at fast-food restaurants?

3. Was it taste, reasons of health, or economy that made the impact?

Fast-food restaurants had better find answers to the above questions fast—faster than the service at the drive-through window. If they don't, the competition will be smiling brightly as they serve the former fast food patrons.

FIGURE 6.4: GRANDPARENTS WHO ARE REGULAR FAST-FOOD PATRONS

Aug-07	Aug-08	Aug-09	Aug-10	Aug-11
33.2%	34.9%	31.8%	30.5%	30.4%

Source: BIGinsight.com

Size matters

Eating out can be a relaxing way to end a stressful day. A beverage can calm the most savage beast, particularly, as you are being served one of your favorite foods.

Size matters in many areas of our lives. Consumers often think that bigger is better. We want to super-size our meals for the extra value. In Chapter 3, we learned about the results of our obsession with buying larger homes. The fast-food industry has a laser-focused goal of continually increasing the number of persons served. The more persons served, the more products consumed, the more loyal customers generated, and the cycle repeats.

Realizing the importance of family size, we asked consumers about the number of persons in the household and if they ate at fast-food restaurants. We wanted to find out if family size influences fast-food restaurant patronage. The answer is "perhaps." Refer to Figure 6.5. Between May 2005 and May 2011, on average and based on these responses, the five-person family unit was the one most likely to regularly eat fast food. The four-person family unit followed closely behind. One fact remains, fast-food restaurants have become increasingly popular with the American consumer—these conglomerates make billions annually.

FIGURE 6.5: REGULAR FAST FOOD EATERS

Number of persons in household	May-05	May-06	May-07	May-08	May-09	May-10	May-11
1	46.1%	37.9%	38.2%	36.1%	35.4%	32.1%	31.4%
2	47.5%	39.2%	37.6%	35.5%	36.6%	33.7%	34.2%
3	55.5%	45.5%	42.7%	42.0%	44.8%	43.9%	39.9%
4	56.3%	37.1%	45.4%	46.5%	45.7%	42.6%	44.3%
5	58.7%	45.7%	45.3%	43.2%	41.2%	41.0%	44.1%

Source: BIGinsight.com

Catering to the minor leagues

Ronald McDonald, Wendy the cute, red-headed girl, the Taco Bell chihuahua dog, Burger King's character of a king, and Chick-fil-A's cow are all symbols of fun—humorous with a sense of innocence.

The mascots are attractive to adults but definitely translate to young children. Make no mistake, however, the fast-food industry may seem as if they are catering to the minor leagues (those under eighteen) but the majority of the target market remains adults.

During May 2005, regardless of the number of persons in the household under the age of eighteen, anywhere from 47.6% to 59.6% of consumers surveyed regularly ate at fast-food restaurants (Figure 6.6). It looks as if families of all sizes chose to dine using paper, plastic, and a straw. When the economy crashed in 2008, consumers nationwide were hurting. Foreclosures, employee lay-offs, unemployment, and a roller-coaster stock market continued to make headlines. With such a challenging economy, it would have been logical to assume that families would cut back on dining out. And this was true for all families. By 2011, family dining via a drive-through window continued to decline. These are the probable explanations for consumers' revolt against the fast-food purveyors:

- It is more cost effective to prepare food at home.

- It is healthier to prepare food at home.

- Cooking as an "art" or hobby has become more popular.

Regardless of the reason, consumers' patronage over the years declined. Does this mean that fast-food restaurants will soon be extinct? Absolutely not. But these statistics do help explain fast-food restaurants aggressive product and advertising decisions, such as:

- Serving fruit, yogurt, and oatmeal in order to drive in business from health-conscious consumers

- Interior decors being updated to look more like a café

- Seasonal products (for example, the flavors of milkshakes) being offered to stimulate impulse purchases.

FIGURE 6.6: NUMBER OF PERSONS UNDER EIGHTEEN IN
REGULAR FAST FOOD EATER HOUSEHOLDS

Number of persons in household under 18	May-05	May-06	May-07	May-08	May-09	May-10	May-11
0	47.6%	38.6%	38.5%	37.7%	37.8%	34.7%	34.1%
1	58.7%	45.8%	49.4%	44.2%	48.2%	44.4%	43.6%
2	58.5%	43.9%	44.0%	44.4%	42.7%	45.5%	46.9%
3	57.9%	44.2%	44.3%	41.4%	39.8%	38.2%	44.1%
4	59.6%	48.9%	54.4%	52.3%	46.4%	40.8%	36.6%
5	48.5%	39.0%	43.8%	28.4%	32.5%	38.8%	32.0%

Source: BIGinsight.com

Who is being served through a window?

Any way you cut the French fries, it is obvious that consumers enjoy fast food. Sure McDonald's serves oatmeal. Taco Bell insists that real beef is used as part of the ingredients. Milk is part of the 650 calorie milkshake at Burger King. Despite the "healthy" ingredients, the negative aspects of fast food still go to our hips and our blood vessels.

But this book isn't about nutrition; this book is about consumers' behaviors. We have learned the young and old, single and married all gather to get quick meals in a box, bag, or on a tray at fast-food restaurants. The next realm to venture into is "the most popular fast food restaurants." In May 2011, we asked consumers which restaurant they ate at most regularly. Figure 6.7 shows us that women in our sample were the dominant fast food visitors. There is also a clear cut "winner" in terms of a favorite fast-food restaurant—McDonald's. Wendy's, Burger King, Subway, and Taco Bell each received approximately the same level of preference. Arby's came in last indicating it's not as popular of a choice for patrons. Of the six restaurants identified, only Taco Bell offered a menu different from the traditional burger and fries. Yet the preference level did not change significantly. This could also mean that the food doesn't really matter; it's time, convenience, and location above all.

FIGURE 6.7: FREQUENT FAST FOOD PATRONS BY GENDER

	May-09		May-10		May-11	
	Male	Female	Male	Female	Male	Female
McDonald's	29.0%	31.7%	29.4%	35.0%	31.8%	35.5%
Wendy's	10.7%	9.7%	9.6%	8.5%	9.1%	10.6%
Burger King	7.1%	8.2%	11.1%	7.2%	8.7%	5.2%
Subway	7.1%	5.6%	6.1%	6.6%	7.4%	6.7%
Taco Bell	8.3%	8.6%	7.8%	8.6%	6.8%	7.5%
Arby's	3.4%	2.4%	2.3%	2.1%	2.4%	2.4%

Source: BIGinsight.com

Summary

The next time someone asks, "What's for dinner?" there is a good chance the answer is a burger, fries, and a coke. Fast-food restaurants have found the secret formula for bringing in consumers regardless of age. The advertisements and mascots may cater to children, but the primary target market of these food purveyors is adults. Married couples ate regularly at Ronald's house, across the border, or with the King.

Top five lessons learned

1. Consumers continue to eat fast food despite the calories, carbohydrates, sugar, and heavy advertising campaigns regarding their evils.

2. Men and women are equally prone to grab a burger, fries, and soda through a fast-food window. Neither sex has a reason to act superior when talking about their restraint from eating fast food.

3. Single people are the primary patrons of fast-food restaurants.

4. Fast-food advertisements may cater to young children, but the dominant consumer is over eighteen years old.

5. There is also a clear cut "winner" in terms of a favorite fast-food restaurant — McDonald's.

References

Centers for Disease Control and Prevention. "Percent of Adults Age 20 years and Over Who Are Obese." (2007-2008) Retrieved February 8, 2011 from http://www.cdc.gov/nchs/fastats/overwt.htm.

Dunne, P. M. and R. F. Lusch. *Retailing.* Cengage Learning, Florence, KY, 2007.

IB Times Staff Reporter. "68 Percent Americans Found to Be Overweight as Obesity Becomes Global Epidemic." *International Business Times* (February 4, 2011) Retrieved February 8, 2011 from http://www.ibtimes.com/articles/108770/20110204/u-s-americans-obesity-bmi-body-mass-risk-factor-disease.htm

2009 Financial Highlights. McDonald's Corporation. 2009. Retrieved February 8, 2011 from http://www.aboutmcdonalds.com/mcd/investors/publications/2009_Financial_Highlights.html

2009 Financial Highlights. Yum! Brands. 2009. Retrieved February 8, 2011 http://www.yum.com/annualreport/pdf/2009annualreport.pdf

Chapter

7

Clash of the Big Box Retailers

R etailers used to be defined by the products they sold. Department stores sold everything including furniture, clothing, accessories, cosmetics, and shoes for the entire family. Specialty stores offered merchandise in one or a few categories. They also offered a more personal shopping experience. Discounters offered merchandise at a price lower than department stores and specialty stores. Then, as if overnight, large, hulking stores came to pervade the retail industry. Massive buildings were being erected. Instead of the traditional classification, a new category was developed: the "big box store." To date, there are two categories of merchandise for big box stores: general merchandise and specialty stores.

Two examples of big box retailers selling general merchandise are Walmart and Target. Examples of specialty big box retailers include Lowe's and the Home Depot. With an average store size of 130,000 square feet, these retailers are massive. They offer consumers a wide assortment of merchandise, including store and national brands.

There is no doubt that these titans of industry changed the fabric of retailing. As big box companies fight to the finish to attract consumers, the number-one question for the industry remains "What is the consumer profile for each big box retailer?" It would be easy to make assumptions, but, instead, let's look at what the research reveals.

Walmart versus Target

Walmart and Target are similar on three fronts. They are big box retailers and both are considered discounters. The third similarity is based on their level of competition: they are aggressive, seasoned, and highly professional retailers. Multi-billion dollar big box stores became successful by offering consistent pricing, marketing aggressively, maintaining a tight control on all company policies, and delivering what they believed to be the perfect level of customer service.

Sam Walton started Walmart based on an "everyday low price" strategy. This strategy is targeted toward low- to middle-income families. A few years ago, Walmart decided that they were going to compete directly with Target. The company dropped the everyday low price strategy, changed the merchandise categories carried, widened the aisles, and marketed the company differently. After poor sales, the company went back to the everyday low price strategy (todaysthv.com, 2011). The changed strategy suggested that the two big box retailers, while offering general merchandise, catered to very different target markets.

Walmart's realization that its original strategy was better for the company demonstrated that all big box stores are not alike. Companies may be significantly different based on their target market and their consumers' needs and wants. As of July 2011, Walmart and Target attracted a heavy percent of female shoppers—more than 60% of the shoppers at both retailers were female (Figure 7.1). The products, advertising, and overall marketing mix were successful in attracting women customers. In addition, the majority of consumers were married. But let's look a bit more closely. Target also attracted 23% of the single crowd.

FIGURE 7.1: WOMEN'S CLOTHING SHOPPERS

	Walmart	Target
Gender		
Male	36.8%	36.0%
Female	63.2%	64.0%
Marital status		
Married	54.5%	54.5%
Living with partner	11.1%	10.9%
Divorced or separated	14.1%	6.2%
Widowed	5.4%	5.5%
Single, never married	14.9%	23.0%
Age		
18-24	7.4%	11.8%
25-34	14.2%	30.1%
35-44	21.9%	19.6%
45-54	27.9%	14.7%
55-64	14.4%	14.4%
65 and older	15.0%	9.5%
Average age	46.9	41.5
Annual total income of household		
Less than $15,000	20.7%	14.1%
$15,000 to $24,999	19.4%	11.1%
$25,000 to $34,999	20.6%	19.0%
$35,000 to $49,999	15.7%	14.1%
$50,000 to $74,999	16.8%	30.4%
$75,000 to $99,999	5.6%	11.6%
$100,000 to $149,000	2.2%	2.9%
$150,000 or more	0.4%	0.9%
Average income	$36,458	$47,163

Source: BIGinsight.com

Walmart has an older customer—the average being 46.9. Target's average customer was 41.5 years old. Target's newest emphasis has been on "fast fashion," and this tactic has brought in this fashion-oriented, primarily female consumer group. Fast fashion consists of fashionable apparel carried for a maximum of only six to eight weeks. This strategy keeps the merchandise fresh and encourages repeat customer traffic.

The largest difference between these two titans of industry was the annual household income of the consumers they attracted. Those attracted to Walmart's everyday low pricing strategy had an average household income of $36,458. Target customers on the other hand earned an average income of $47,163. Its emphasis on designer labels in home goods and apparel proved more attractive to higher income levels.

These two retailers may be discounters, but the statistics reveal that their target markets were very different, particularly in relation to customers' income. The fact that Walmart had to retreat back to its old everyday low pricing strategy in February 2011 (Wall Street Journal, February 6, 2011) made complete sense when their average customer income was revealed. In tight financial times, I suspect this income bracket consumer appreciated the everyday low pricing strategy.

Lowe's versus the Home Depot

Some jingles stay in your mind for a long time. For many years, one of the most memorable was the Ace Hardware jingle: "Ace is the place with the helpful hardware man!" Back in the 1980s, Ace hired John Madden as its spokesperson. Talk about a "man's man." John Madden was built like a truck, had a winning smile, and was a football star. Ace Hardware is a traditional hardware specialty outlet. A store "Tim the Tool Man" Taylor from the sitcom *Home Improvement* would appreciate. Okay, there is one slight problem. The jingle completely ignores the female target market. Using John Madden as the spokesperson also implies that women have no reason for entering a hardware store. Don't get me wrong, I like John Madden. However—and this is a very big *however*—the message I got from Ace was "My ex-husband is more welcome in Ace than I am, and if I need lawn equipment or a tool, please bring along someone with a healthy dose of testosterone."

Along came two big box stores that wanted in on the hardware and garden action. They smelled money—and lots of it. Lowe's and the Home Depot entered the retailing scene as big box stores. Their retailing footprints dwarfed the size of Ace Hardware stores. The average size of a Lowe's or Home Depot store was 130,000 square feet. That's a lot of lumber, lighting, garden, appliances, and tools. Can there really be enough consumers to keep two big box hardware stores in business? You bet! The keys to success have been (a) keeping their existing target markets happy and (b) expanding the target market. The expansion of the target market during the new millennium has been to women.

According to consumers, the two big box retailers slugging it out to sell hardware and garden supplies are equally attractive to men and women. Lowe's and the Home Depot realize that women are a very desirable and lucrative target market. As shown in Figure 7.2 both titans of power tools attract over 50% of women shoppers. A greater percent of married couples shop at Lowe's (56.1%) compared with the Home Depot (49.2%). The average age of consumers for both stores is relatively similar (47.8 and 45.7, respectively).

Now check out the consumers' income in each target market. The average annual household income of consumers that shop at Lowe's and the Home Depot are within a $2,000 spread. This suggests that both retailers attract a similar target market based on income. These consumers earn report an income well above the national average. The potential for disposable income exist for purchases on lamps, flowers, carpeting, and tools.

The similarities between the stores' target market demographic profiles suggest that intangible services will play a strategic role. Products and merchandise lines can easily be duplicated by each competitor. The quality and depth of services offered may be the deciding factor in building patronage behavior and customer loyalty.

FIGURE 7.2: HOME IMPROVEMENT SHOPPERS

	Lowe's	Home Depot
Gender		
Male	45.7%	47.9%
Female	54.3%	52.1%
Marital status		
Married	56.1%	49.2%
Living with partner	8.9%	9.1%
Divorced or separated	11.0%	11.8%
Widowed	5.7%	4.8%
Single, never married	18.4%	25.1%
Age		
18-24	8.8%	12.8%
25-34	16.0%	15.9%
35-44	17.3%	19.0%
45-54	20.3%	19.9%
55-64	17.8%	15.5%
65 and older	19.8%	17.0%
Average age	47.8	45.7
Annual total income of household		
Less than $15,000	8.0%	9.1%
$15,000 to $24,999	10.7%	10.8%
$25,000 to $34,999	14.6%	14.5%
$35,000 to $49,999	18.8%	17.4%
$50,000 to $74,999	23.9%	21.4%
$75,000 to $99,999	12.4%	13.1%
$100,000 to $149,000	8.5%	9.1%
$150,000 or more	3.2%	4.6%
Average income	$57,326	$59,077

Source: BIGinsight.com

Walmart versus Toys "R" Us versus Target

Toys may be for children, but the toy industry is not for kids, crybabies, or whiners. The toy industry is a rough-and-tumble industry where only the toughest survive. Oh sure, Barbie looks pretty on the outside, but I have it on trustworthy confidential information that she is hard on the inside.

The three big box toy retailers in the U.S. are Walmart, Toys "R" Us, and Target. Geoffrey (the giraffe spokesperson) from Toys "R" Us continues his effort to stomp out Walmart and Target. He presents Toys "R" Us as a fun place to shop where every toy is available. If you have never been in a Toys "R" Us store, I encourage you to go—if only for the experience. It's a bit like having a brain freeze from eating ice cream too fast.

Walmart and Target don't have any cute talking animals as a spokesperson. However, both companies possess a very healthy toy business. Geoffrey the Giraffe will have to get used to the competition.

We asked consumers at which big box store they primarily purchase toys. The profile of the three giants of toys is similar in some ways and different in others. As shown on Figure 7.3, Target attracts the most females (69.9%); the dominant toy shopper at Walmart is also female (62.7%). Toys "R" Us has an equally distributed amount of male and female shoppers (50.7% and 49.3%, respectively).

Toys are purchased as gifts, for immediate family members and for extended family members. One goal of these big box toy retailers is to attract toy consumers regardless of the recipient. The Target customer's marital status often helps the retailer formulate marketing messages, particularly visual messages. In July 2011, a survey of consumers reveals that marital status varies among Walmart, Toys "R" Us, and Target patrons. While the majority of consumers identify themselves as married for each store, differences exist. Toys "R" Us attracts a smaller percentage of married consumers (51.5%). They compensate by drawing in single individuals (25.0%). Target attracts the highest percent of married consumers (58.9%).

The common demographic found among consumers who shop for toys is their average age. Regardless of their favorite big box toy store, the average age is relatively similar (41.8 Target, 43.1 Toys "R" Us, and 43.6 Walmart).

The 24/7 news cycle and talking heads on cable stations provide plenty of information about the challenges of today's economy. The negative talk is justified. Layoffs, unemployment, and rising gas prices are front-page news; consumer discouragement over the economy continues to build. Regardless of the poor state of the economy, if you have children, the purchase of at least one toy periodically is a constant in the budget. In light of this, these three big box retailers continue to differentiate themselves based on price and income than perhaps any other big box retailer.

Review the annual total income of households on Figure 7.3. The income levels of the consumers vary based on the retailer patronized. Consumers who shop primarily at Walmart for toys report an annual household income of $48,010. Those who shop at Toys "R" Us indicate an average income of $62,258. The highest incomes, $66,869, purchase toys at Target.

Walmart has the most distinctive demographic target market among the three big box toy retailers. During the recession in 2008, its low prices brought in consumers that were struggling, had cut back or simply become more strategic in their purchasing behavior.

The demographic profiles of Toys "R" Us and Target are similar. Target however, is able to capitalize on its other product categories. Once in a Target store, the retailer is able to strategically place toys throughout different aisles to encourage impulse purchases. Toys "R" Us requires destination shopping. Consumers must consciously know that they want to look for children's toys.

The success of these three toy titans suggests that they will probably expand their footprints throughout the U.S. They will also continue to fight to the finish in an attempt to gain as much market share as possible. There is a lot of money to be obtained in the toy industry. This is not a game. Losing is not an option. To the victor go the spoils!

FIGURE 7.3: Toys Shoppers

	Walmart	Toys "R" Us	Target
Gender			
Male	37.3%	50.7%	30.1%
Female	62.7%	49.3%	69.9%
Marital status			
Married	57.3%	51.5%	58.9%
Living with partner	10.7%	9.2%	8.7%
Divorced or separated	11.3%	10.6%	7.6%
Widowed	3.9%	3.7%	4.4%
Single, never married	16.8%	25.0%	20.4%
Age			
18-24	10.9%	15.3%	13.5%
25-34	21.3%	21.3%	26.5%
35-44	21.1%	19.5%	21.9%
45-54	22.2%	16.1%	14.6%
55-64	13.6%	14.2%	10.4%
65 and older	10.9%	13.7%	13.1%
Average age	43.6	43.1	41.8
Annual total income of household			
Less than $15,000	13.1%	8.2%	7.0%
$15,000 to $24,999	14.4%	9.4%	7.0%
$25,000 to $34,999	16.5%	13.6%	10.9%
$35,000 to $49,999	18.2%	16.7%	15.1%
$50,000 to $74,999	21.3%	23.1%	26.6%
$75,000 to $99,999	9.7%	13.5%	16.1%
$100,000 to $149,000	5.3%	10.1%	12.0%
$150,000 or more	1.6%	5.5%	5.4%
Average income	$48,010	$62,258	$66,869

Source: BIGinsight.com

Best Buy versus Circuit City

It would be irresponsible to have a chapter on big box stores without addressing electronics. I often think recent events in the electronics industry are comparable to a boxing match. Mike Tyson's infamous ear biting will go down in history. It may even overshadow all his great accomplishments as a boxer. Similarly, the complete annihilation of Circuit City will also overshadow all of the successes the company achieved.

Best Buy and Circuit City were without a doubt the two largest and most formidable big box electronic companies in the U.S. Best Buy featured blue and gold colors, while Circuit City sported red and black colors. Consumers simply needed to remember the colors to find their favorite electronics retailer.

The saying what goes up must come down was very true for Circuit City. The company was once the second-largest electronics big box retailer in the U.S. By 2009, the company had generated so much debt it had no choice but to liquidate. The company was wiped out (Reisinger, 2009).

And then there was one. Best Buy stands alone. In 2011, Best Buy was the only big box electronics retailer. Before you jump out of your seat, yes, Walmart and Target do sell electronics. However, Best Buy was the single big box retailer that *only* sold electronics. This company made a unique niche for themselves comparable to Toys "R" Us. The difference was that consumers were obsessed, dare I say, addicted to electronics. Furthermore, consumers of all ages wanted, needed, dreamed of, and planned for their next electronic upgrade or purchase.

Consumers who shop at Best Buy are equally divided between male and female (51.0%, 49.0%, respectively) (Figure 7.4). The retailer attracts couples who were married (51%), or living together (9.7%), as well as those who are single (24.4%). Being the only big box electronics retailer, they attract consumers of all ages—the average being 45.2.

FIGURE 7.4: Electronics Shoppers

	Best Buy Shoppers
Gender	
Male	51.0%
Female	49.0%
Marital status	
Married	51.0%
Living with partner	9.7%
Divorced or separated	10.6%
Widowed	4.3%
Single, never married	24.4%
Age	
18-24	12.9%
25-34	17.5%
35-44	18.7%
45-54	19.3%
55-64	16.0%
65 and older	15.6%
Average age	45.2
Annual total income of household	
Less than $15,000	7.3%
$15,000 to $24,999	9.6%
$25,000 to $34,999	12.9%
$35,000 to $49,999	17.7%
$50,000 to $74,999	23.5%
$75,000 to $99,999	14.1%
$100,000 to $149,000	10.2%
$150,000 or more	4.7%
Average income	$62,023

Source: BIGinsight.com

Electronics can be classified as a high-ticket item. High-definition TVs, computers, and cameras can easily cost thousands of dollars. The average annual total household income of our survey was $62,023. These consumers are classified well above the national average. Of course, these shoppers may still be placing high-ticket items on credit cards—debt just a swipe of the credit card away. Should the economy continue to suffer, the company may find consumers wanting to find electronics for a lower price elsewhere. But where?

Summary

Big box companies entered the U.S. landscape and have permanently changed the retail industry footprint. Enormous buildings with high ceilings, cement floors, and twelve-foot-high shelves display thousands of products. Big box retailers have learned that regardless of the product, female shoppers were influential in the shopping process and final purchase decision.

Regardless of gender, marital status, or age, the bottom line for these titans of retail was financial. The primary difference between many of the competing big box retailers was the consumer's annual household income. The question retailers should continually ask themselves is "Was my marketing effort attractive to the income level of my target market?"

Top five lessons learned

1. Walmart and Target dominate in multiple categories as big box retailers.

2. The female customer is important to the hardware industry.

3. The demographics of the Lowe's and the Home Depot consumer are similar.

4. Toy big box retailers (Walmart, Toys "R" Us, Target) cater to different income brackets.

5. Best Buy consumers had a high average income ($62,023).

References

Reisinger, Dan. "Circuit City: A Eulogy." *The Digital Home* (January 19, 2009) Retrieved March 11, 2011 from http://news.cnet.com/circuit-city-a-eulogy/?tag=mncol;txt

Today's THV.com. "After Slumping Sales, Walmart Goes Back to Basics." (February 24, 2011) Retrieved March 7, 2011 from http://www.todaysthv.com/news/arkbus/ story.aspx?storyid=145854

Wall Street Journal. "Walmart, Humbled King of Retail, Plots Rebound." (February 6, 2011) Retrieved March 10, 2011 from http://online.wsj.com/article/APe52e41e9d3574b2487905450ab24dcf.html?KEYWORDS=walmart+everyday +low+pricing+strategy

Chapter

8

Shopping in Your Boxers, Briefs, or Bathrobe

The catalog is the oldest form of direct marketing. It also continues to be very popular with customers and profitable for companies. It seems as if you can purchase almost anything from a catalog from the ever so popular Victoria's Secret's push-up bra to hunting and fishing gear by Bass.

As technology evolved, so too did direct marketing. Catalog retailing paved the way for the TV shopping networks. In the beginning, some of the brick-and-mortar retailers may have dismissed these electronic retailers. I certainly received many questions from retailers and consumers. Questions usually revolved around the credibility of the promotional efforts. Are the TV shopping networks really selling as much merchandise as the counter indicates? Are the products really as good as the testimonials suggested? Can I trust purchasing something through a "television program"?

For the trifecta of shopping in your boxers, briefs, or bathrobe, online shopping was introduced. Twenty years ago consumers were concerned about releasing their credit card information to online retailers. Many brick-and-mortar retailers were sans an online presence. In 2011, consumers can purchase clothing, hardware, and even order groceries via the Internet. If you can't get something in the U.S., simply order it internationally. If you have a credit card, delivery address, and a computer with access to the Internet, you can purchase almost anything.

Catalog shoppers

Before the Internet, children looked forward to the Sears Christmas wish book. It was bigger than a phone book and offered all the wonders a child could want. For adults with a substantial income, the Neiman Marcus Christmas catalog could make even the most jaded billionaire squeal with delight.

Before catalog retailers choose which products to feature in the catalog, they often ask "Who are the decision makers?" and "Who makes the actual catalog purchase?" Based on surveys between February 2004 and February 2011, BIGinsight developed a profile of consumers who expressed the intention to shop via catalog more often during the next ninety days. Let's see how this consumer profile has modified over the period.

FIGURE 8.1: DEMOGRAPHIC PROFILE OF CONSUMERS WHO PLAN TO USE CATALOGS MORE OVER THE NEXT 90 DAYS

	Feb-04	Feb-05	Feb-06	Feb-07	Feb-08	Feb-09	Feb-10	Feb-11
Gender								
Men	50.1%	47.8%	37.4%	36.5%	41.4%	49.6%	56.7%	53.9%
Women	49.9%	52.2%	62.6%	63.5%	58.6%	50.4%	43.3%	46.1%
Marital status								
Married	36.0%	40.8%	48.3%	42.2%	45.7%	42.9%	49.0%	42.2%

	Feb-04	Feb-05	Feb-06	Feb-07	Feb-08	Feb-09	Feb-10	Feb-11
Living with partner	11.3%	29.2%	15.9%	13.6%	12.8%	8.2%	4.1%	13.2%
Divorced or separated	16.3%	9.3%	11.0%	9.1%	11.1%	12.2%	7.8%	7.0%
Widowed	2.9%	3.3%	4.1%	5.5%	3.4%	3.6%	2.9%	2.2%
Single, never married	33.4%	17.4%	20.8%	29.5%	26.9%	33.1%	36.2%	35.4%
Age								
18-24	14.5%	31.2%	18.3%	24.5%	19.5%	21.6%	24.3%	26.1%
25-34	32.3%	22.9%	18.3%	25.0%	21.3%	15.5%	18.2%	30.2%
35-44	21.0%	19.3%	27.7%	14.3%	19.4%	17.9%	23.5%	14.9%
45-54	16.8%	10.9%	19.7%	19.4%	17.1%	17.4%	15.4%	13.6%
55-64	5.4%	6.9%	6.9%	10.8%	10.8%	14.4%	11.6%	8.5%
65+	10.0%	8.7%	9.0%	6.1%	11.9%	13.3%	7.0%	6.7%
Average age	39.3	36.5	40.3	38.4	41.2	42.6	39.1	36.7
Income								
Less than $15,000	17.4%	20.1%	14.4%	12.2%	12.6%	17.6%	15.6%	13.4%
$15,000 to $24,999	21.5%	5.0%	7.7%	8.2%	10.3%	9.2%	7.3%	13.2%
$25,000 to $34,999	13.6%	12.1%	14.9%	14.7%	12.4%	16.6%	17.4%	11.5%
$35,000 to $49,999	20.3%	20.4%	24.5%	18.2%	17.2%	13.1%	17.5%	19.6%
$50,000 to $74,999	17.7%	23.6%	19.6%	22.5%	23.7%	17.5%	18.0%	17.6%
$75,000 to $99,999	3.4%	7.2%	9.0%	8.9%	11.7%	8.9%	4.2%	11.5%
$100,000 to $149,999	4.4%	5.6%	3.3%	5.9%	8.8%	8.8%	12.3%	8.0%
$150,000 or more	1.8%	6.0%	6.6%	9.3%	3.4%	8.4%	7.7%	5.3%
Average income	$41,296	$53,804	$53,613	$60,522	$56,307	$58,480	$59,565	$56,006

Source: BIGinsight.com

As revealed in Figure 8.1, the genders' use of catalogs between 2004 and 2011 looks like a roller-coaster ride offered at Disney World. Users start out relatively stable, go up, down, and then level out. In February 2004, the *gender of catalog* users was relatively even with 50.1% male and 49.9% female consumers. By 2007, females dominated the catalog purchasing with 63.5% versus 36.5%. Finally in 2011, the use of catalogs by both genders leveled out with men using them more (53.9%) as compared to females (46.1%).

Catalogs offer consumers greater flexibility in shopping during non-store hours. This form of shopping is specifically geared to people with challenging schedules; *married consumers* for example. In February 2004, 36% of the sample is married. By 2007, 42% are married. This figure remains the same through 2011. It makes sense that as consumers' lives become more complicated, they add shopping conveniences to their schedule.

Understanding the *age* of the catalog shopper is very important. It influences the overall image of the catalog presentation, marketing messages used, and products included. In 2004, the average age of the consumer who plans to shop more with catalogs was 39. Three years later, the age changed only by one year to 38. In 2011, the average age of the consumer was 36. The young age of the catalog consumer is exciting and important to catalog retailers. Their young age suggests that they have a long lifetime of consumption ahead of them. Catalog retailers may be able to secure these retailers as loyal customers for twenty or thirty additional years.

Age isn't the only demographic to be excited about regarding this consumer. As we look at their *income*, we learn that these shoppers earn above the national average. In February 2004, the reported income was $41,296. By 2011, the average income of this catalog shopper was $56,006. If (and this is a big if) the consumer is debt free, he or she has discretionary income to spend on catalog purchases.

TV shoppers

If you made a friendly bet about which gender spends more time and/or money shopping via TV retailers, are you confident you would win? We'll reveal the unexpected answer soon. First, a bit of background.

The two biggest TV shopping channels are QVC and HSN. They may be the biggest, but think about all the other products that are sold through the TV. Remember the commercial about the Snuggie? I laugh each time I see people wrapped up in a blanket. The developer of the Snuggie laughs all the way to the bank as viewers order the sleeved blanket for aunts, uncles, cousins, brothers, and pets. The Magic Bullet blender continues to fly off the warehouse shelves as TV viewers watch delicious food items being made in under a minute. Does any of this ring a bell?

Now that many consumers own HDTV, 52-inch flat-screens, and "man caves," it is even easier to spend more time in front of the television. Personally, I don't know how I functioned before I had my flat-screen TV—but that is another story. The advanced television technology has made it more entertaining to watch TV and shop simultaneously.

It is time to answer the question at the beginning of this section: "Which gender shops more through the TV?" In February 2004, males and females had approximately the same TV shopping practices (50.7% versus 49.3% respectively) (Figure 8.2). By 2007, females took the lead in TV shopping with 52%. Something inexplicable happens in 2011. The TV shopping world shifts. In February 2011, we asked men and women if they plan to shop more or less via TV in the next ninety days; 67.1% of the men stated that they planned to shop more via TV compared with 32.9% of women. Perhaps shopping via the TV is becoming more enticing to men due to the invention of the "man cave." Maybe it is the result of bigger and better TVs. Maybe it is the result of more TV channels;

perhaps men simply don't like shopping malls. Regardless of the reason, men's intentions to shop at home while watching TV appear to be on the rise. Wow! More power to men and retailers selling through TV.

The *marital status* of the TV shopper is similar to the catalog shopper. In February 2004, 36.8% of the sample was married. This percent grew slightly to 37.2% in 2007. The real increase is in 2011, with 46% of the sample married. This figure is similar to that of catalog shoppers.

The TV shopper is relatively young, in his or her thirties. In February 2004, the consumer's *average age* was 38.8. By 2011, the average age is 33. This young shopper may be shopping via TV after work, during the early hours, or on the weekend. Regardless, the TV shopping retailers have a consumer target market that is relatively young and can be developed into a lifelong loyal consumer.

Similar to the catalog shopper, the TV shopper's *income* was above the national average. In February 2004, TV shopping retailers attract consumers with an average income of $41,559. This average increased to $67,044 by 2007. By February 2011, the average income declined to $59,783. Yes indeed, these TV shoppers are male, young, and married. Despite the fluctuation in income, this group is well above the national average.

FIGURE 8.2: Demographic Profile of Consumers Who Planned to Shop More Via the TV in the Next 90 Days

	Feb-04	Feb-05	Feb-06	Feb-07	Feb-08	Feb-09	Feb-10	Feb-11
Gender								
Men	50.7%	32.0%	55.2%	48.0%	65.5%	61.0%	76.0%	67.1%
Women	49.3%	68.0%	44.8%	52.0%	34.5%	39.0%	24.0%	32.9%
Marital status								
Married	36.8%	40.8%	35.2%	37.2%	31.4%	49.2%	42.7%	46.0%
Living with partner	12.7%	14.7%	21.4%	8.3%	20.3%	5.1%	2.4%	4.9%

	Feb-04	Feb-05	Feb-06	Feb-07	Feb-08	Feb-09	Feb-10	Feb-11
Divorced or separated	14.6%	12.0%	19.1%	15.0%	2.8%	3.7%	2.0%	6.7%
Widowed	2.8%	1.2%	0.7%	11.6%	0.8%	0.0%	1.5%	2.7%
Single, never married	33.0%	31.3%	23.5%	27.8%	44.6%	42.0%	51.4%	39.7%
Age								
18-24	12.3%	18.5%	23.6%	26.5%	30.2%	29.3%	39.7%	35.0%
25-34	36.6%	19.4%	20.4%	24.4%	30.1%	22.6%	26.2%	36.0%
35-44	21.5%	29.3%	30.7%	15.0%	27.8%	24.7%	7.9%	10.6%
45-54	14.7%	19.2%	16.6%	21.8%	5.8%	9.0%	15.1%	7.9%
55-64	6.5%	8.9%	4.5%	9.1%	4.0%	11.0%	9.3%	3.8%
65+	8.3%	4.7%	4.2%	3.1%	2.1%	3.4%	1.8%	6.6%
Average age	38.8	39.2	36.9	37.1	32.9	35.9	33.4	33.0
Income								
Less than $15,000	13.6%	19.1%	20.5%	9.1%	16.1%	35.5%	19.3%	14.4%
$15,000 to $24,999	35.3%	2.5%	8.2%	10.4%	14.8%	9.6%	13.0%	7.3%
$25,000 to $34,999	10.2%	19.7%	15.8%	18.8%	15.7%	5.8%	22.6%	12.9%
$35,000 to $49,999	7.8%	26.7%	18.1%	12.5%	15.5%	12.6%	21.4%	18.2%
$50,000 to $74,999	22.9%	9.8%	12.6%	22.2%	24.6%	15.4%	12.7%	20.4%
$75,000 to $99,999	3.4%	16.8%	9.7%	2.4%	3.7%	7.3%	3.7%	10.9%
$100,000 to $149,999	4.9%	5.4%	0.0%	12.1%	6.6%	11.6%	3.8%	9.8%
$150,000 or more	1.9%	0.0%	15.1%	12.6%	2.9%	2.2%	3.5%	6.1%
Average income	$41,559	$47,210	$58,934	$67,044	$47,881	$46,903	$42,427	$59,783

Online shopping

Online shopping is big business. In less than two decades, online shopping has shaken the retailing world. Companies that once stated, "no online presence for us," are now offering multiple channels in which consumers can purchase merchandise. How important is online retailing? During the 2010 holiday season, online retailing accounted for 15.4% of overall retail sales (Zimmerman, 2010). This number is making online retailers grin from ear to ear. If you are wondering what the big hoopla is all about, Forrester stated that in 2009 online retail sales accounted for just 7% of overall retail sales. In any type of economy, this jump is excellent. In a recession, this jump is phenomenal.

There are several explanations for consumers' acceptance of online shopping. Reliable credit card security is the first reason. Free shipping during the holiday season is the second reason. However, these two reasons alone won't keep consumers online. Changes in the economy, weather, and national branding are helping online retailers maintain an upward trajectory.

If we look at the other reasons for the big acceptance in online shopping, the first is the *economy*. Consumers continue to enjoy their bigger cars, SUVs, and minivans. The two-vehicle family is common throughout the land (and add another vehicle if the family has teenagers). As gas prices continue to fluctuate, this makes a significant dent in the family budget. Thus, 22.5% of consumers earning less than $100,000 and 22.1% of consumers in households earning $100,000 or more stated that they shop online more as a result of fluctuating gas prices.

The *weather* during recent years was also a contributing factor for increased online sales. Meteorologists have been on high alert during the past year. Southern states were scorched in the spring and summer months. To ring in the New Year, these same states received a very uncharacteristic ice storm. Dramatic changes in the weather often result in consumers avoiding shopping and strip malls. The Internet, however, is just a click away. During the hot and humid summer months, consumers can cool off by the pool and surf their favorite boutique. As winter winds whip through the rafters, they can warm their toes by the fire and purchase parkas, mittens, and ski masks from a multitude of online websites.

National brands sold throughout the Internet were a further contributing factor for rising online sales. Fluctuating gas prices are influencing the number of shopping trips consumers are willing to take. December 2010 data revealed that of consumers in households earning less than $100,000 42.3% indicated that they take fewer shopping trips, while 31.2% of consumers in households earning $100,000 or more said the same. Both groups are, however, doing a significant amount of shopping online (26% and 22.4%, respectively).

The breadth and depth of national brands offered through the Internet have made a significant impact on consumers' purchasing behaviors. The quality and sizing of national brands remain relatively stable. Once a consumer adopts a national brand, he or she will continue to purchase the brand. Consumers are more prone to purchase national brands via the Internet than unknown brands.

It is important to have an understanding of the demographic profile of the online shopper. *Gender* of the online shopper is shown in Figure 8.3. In February 2004, 60.1% of the online shoppers are male and 39.9% are female. The shopping gender profile changes significantly by 2007. Males represent 58.2% of the online shoppers, whereas females represent 41.8%. The gender profile remains relatively stable through February 2011. Males continue to dominate online shopping (56.6%) compared with females (43.4%).

The *marital status* of the online shopper falls into two groups: those who are married and those who are single. The size of the two groups is significant enough to be important to online retailers. In February 2004, 43.8% of online shoppers are married, and 28.3% are single.

By 2007, the percent of married online shoppers remain relatively stable at 43. 8%, but the single online shoppers increase to 34.9%. In 2011, the percent of married online shoppers increase to 45.8%, single online shoppers decrease to 31.7%.

Two variables: a married person plus online shopping. One variable (being married) equates to a very busy life. Online shopping provides an avenue for increased product offering while minimizing the time required to shop. It doesn't take a rocket scientist to understand why married consumers like this form of shopping.

The *average age* of the online shopper is in the late thirties. In February 2004, the average age of the online shopper was 40. By 2011, the average age was 39.3. Check out the *income* level of the online shopper. In 2004, the average income level was $50,204. This figure jumps to $65,615 in 2007. February 2009 reveals the highest income at $99,998. By February 2011, consumers who intend to shop more online in the next ninety days reported an average income slide down to $57,437. This decline in income from 2007 to 2011 is obvious since the economic meltdown of 2008. Despite the economic woes, these consumers' income is well above the national average; they have the ability to shop in general and online.

FIGURE 8.3: DEMOGRAPHIC PROFILE OF CONSUMER WHO INTEND TO SHOP MORE ONLINE IN THE NEXT 90 DAYS

	Feb-04	Feb-05	Feb-06	Feb-07	Feb-08	Feb-09	Feb-10	Feb-11
Gender								
Male	60.1%	55.2%	60.7%	58.2%	56.4%	61.3%	61.0%	56.6%
Female	39.9%	44.8%	39.3%	41.8%	43.6%	38.7%	39.0%	43.4%
Marital Status								
Married	43.9%	45.9%	39.5%	43.8%	43.8%	48.0%	41.1%	45.8%
Living with partner	14.2%	10.5%	10.9%	11.9%	12.2%	9.9%	11.3%	11.2%

	Feb-04	Feb-05	Feb-06	Feb-07	Feb-08	Feb-09	Feb-10	Feb-11
Divorced or separated	12.1%	12.5%	12.1%	7.8%	11.8%	9.9%	7.5%	9.2%
Widowed	1.5%	3.2%	2.3%	1.7%	2.4%	2.8%	2.1%	2.1%
Single, never married	28.3%	27.9%	35.2%	34.9%	29.9%	29.4%	38.1%	31.7%
Age								
18-24	19.2%	16.7%	22.6%	27.4%	23.7%	20.1%	27.0%	20.8%
25-34	21.9%	22.2%	21.8%	22.3%	19.1%	21.6%	20.6%	26.1%
35-44	22.9%	21.7%	22.4%	16.3%	18.0%	18.5%	16.8%	17.8%
45-54	17.9%	20.6%	16.0%	17.8%	19.0%	18.5%	16.1%	16.7%
55-64	10.2%	10.0%	8.9%	9.8%	10.8%	12.2%	11.6%	10.0%
65+	7.9%	8.8%	8.3%	6.3%	9.5%	9.1%	7.8%	8.6%
Average age	40.0	40.9	39.0	37.8	40.1	40.7	38.7	39.3
Income								
Less than $15,000	11.2%	10.3%	11.7%	7.2%	10.0%	8.8%	11.8%	11.2%
$15,000 to $24,999	19.2%	11.0%	12.2%	8.6%	9.3%	10.5%	10.9%	10.6%
$25,000 to $34,999	13.1%	19.2%	13.9%	12.8%	11.9%	10.2%	10.9%	11.8%
$35,000 to $49,999	16.0%	15.6%	18.3%	19.3%	15.2%	14.3%	16.0%	18.1%
$50,000 to $74,999	21.3%	20.5%	17.7%	20.0%	23.8%	21.7%	21.1%	23.3%
$75,000 to $99,999	10.0%	9.8%	14.3%	14.0%	15.7%	13.9%	11.9%	13.2%
$100,000 to $149,999	7.00%	8.80%	7.10%	10.5%	10.7%	13.7%	10.4%	7.70%
$150,000 or more	2.10%	4.70%	4.80%	7.50%	3.50%	6.90%	7.00%	4.20%
Average income	$50,204	$56,292	$56,375	$65,615	$60,908	$66,998	$62,190	$57,437

Source: BIGinsight.com

Summary

Shopping at home is *big* business. Catalogs, TV shopping, and online shopping all offer consumers the opportunity to browse and purchase at home in their boxers, briefs, or bathrobe. Consumers revealed that they enjoy their home shopping activities. The profile of catalog shoppers, TV shopping consumers, and online shoppers are relatively similar. Oh sure, minor differences are revealed, but the differences are indeed minor.

In 2011, the catalog shopper profile is male or female, married, 36 years old, and earned an average income of $56,002. The TV shopper consumer profile is male, married, 33 years old, and earns an average income of $59,783. The online shopper is male or female, married, 39.3 years old, and earns $57,437.

Top five lessons learned

1. Consumers who shop from home earn well above the national average income.

2. Catalog, TV, and online shoppers are young: in their thirties to early forties.

3. Over 40% of the consumers who shop at home are married.

4. Singles comprise 28–35% of consumers who shop at home.

5. Men are the dominant TV shopper.

References

Leggatt, Helen. "Forrester: Growth Forecast for 2009 Online Retail Sales." (January 30, 2009) Retrieved January 13, 2011 from http://www.bizreport.com/2009/01/forrester_growth_forecast_for_2009_online_retail_sales.html#

Zimmerman, Ann. "Gift Shoppers Flocked to the Web." *Wall Street Journal* (December 24, 2010) B1.

Chapter

9

The Way We Communicate

It is hard to imagine now what it was like when cell phones first came on the market. They were the size of a brick (literally). A caller would probably use a landline phone because so few people owned a cell phone. Of course, back then we never even differentiated phones by landline and cell phone. Everyone automatically assumed the phone was a landline.

We communicated face to face or on the traditional phone. We wrote letters and posted them in the U.S. mail, and typed correspondence on a typewriter. Bill Gates and Steve Jobs changed the world when they gave us Microsoft and Apple. What perhaps no one, maybe not even the techies of the world, realized, was that the way we communicate would change at such an amazing rate. The dictionary would need to be constantly updated as new words and phrases were invented to keep up with the advance of technology.

Call me!

As a full-time academic at a large research institution, I am surrounded by 28,000 undergraduate and graduate students on a daily basis. If they aren't calling or texting someone, their phone is in their hands—just in case their BFF (Best Friend Forever) needs to tell them something vital. It is almost impossible to think that in this new millennium anyone would be without a cell phone. But, alas, I work with a faculty member who not only doesn't have a cell phone, he doesn't want a cell phone. His stance on the issue is if anyone wants to get hold of him, the person can call him on his landline. When he told me this I am sure I looked at him as if he was from Mars.

We decided to find out how many consumers are connected by cell phone versus landline. We segmented consumers by age: 18–34, 35–54, and 55 and older. Check out Figure 9.1. In each age category, cell phones are used by 84% or more of the consumers surveyed. There is an indirect relationship between age and the adoption of a cell phone. Younger consumers are more prone to adopt the technology; 14.6% of persons 55 and older don't have a cell phone and don't plan on adopting this technology. This may be older consumers, say over seventy-five, who are more comfortable with landline phones. The faculty member that I mentioned earlier is only 62, but he simply doesn't see any use in the technology. Moral of this information: Every consumer has a preference.

FIGURE 9.1: CELL PHONE USE

Do you have a cell phone?	18–34	35–54	55+
Yes	87.2%	86.6%	84.1%
No, but planning to buy one	3.6%	2.0%	1.3%
No	9.2%	11.5%	14.6%

Source: BIGinsight.com

Business or pleasure?

Now that we know that the majority of consumers own a cell phone. The question remains, "What is the primary purpose of the cell phone?" When cell phones first came on the market, many consumers convinced themselves they "needed" the product for emergencies only. It was beneficial when traveling and emergencies. Little would anyone realize that in a few short years consumers would be using cell phones as a camera, to access the Internet, play music, send text messages, and more.

We asked consumers about their primary use of their cell phone (refer to Figure 9.2). Regardless of age, in excess of 90% use the cell phone mainly for personal use. Consumers aged 35–54 use cell phones the most for business (9.7%). Consumers no longer need to convince themselves that the phone is only for emergencies. We use phones to communicate, chat, gab, and just plain pass the time while waiting in line at the grocery store.

FIGURE 9.2: PRIMARY USE OF CELL PHONE

	18–34	35–54	55+
Business	6.5%	9.7%	7.3%
Personal	93.5%	90.3%	92.7%

Source: BIGinsight.com

Can you commit?

Phone companies are a lot like marriage counselors and the divorce courts. They offer you advice regarding commitment and the penalties associated with breaking up. For example, consumers who aren't afraid of a two-year commitment can receive a better phone bill rate. If you break your commitment, you pay a fee (much like lawyer fees).

For consumers who don't use a phone on a regular basis (the military, for example), a prepaid service is offered. Then for true commitment-phobic consumers, a monthly plan with no contract is offered. Granted, these consumers pay a higher phone bill rate but the cancellation is easier than the contract plan.

Take a look at Figure 9.3. With an excess of 66% of the consumers, a contract plan with a monthly bill is by far the most popular plan regardless of age. Interestingly, as consumers age a greater percentage prefers the prepaid service where you pay for the minutes you use. This suggests that this group of consumers does not use the cell phone to a great extent.

FIGURE 9.3: TYPE OF PLAN

	18–34	35–54	55+
Contract plan with a monthly bill	76.1%	70.3%	66.7%
Prepaid service where you pay for the minutes you use	12.5%	17.2%	20.6%
Monthly plan with no contract where you pay at the beginning of each month	11.4%	12.6%	12.7%

Source: BIGinsight.com

How much?!

There are three groups of consumers. The first group consists of consumers who count every single penny, nickel, and dime while neither spending any of the money nor enjoying many of the things money can buy. The second group consists of consumers that blindly go through life throwing money into the wind. They enjoy the purchasing process, can't understand why they are continually in debt, and don't understand why "there is never enough money." The third group consists of those who monitor the cost of products and services, monitor the inflow and outgo of their money, and, therefore, can enjoy some of the wonderful products offered by retailers.

Cell phone providers promote the different features offered, the phone style, or the ability to receive service from different locations. All of these marketing "talking points" may be attractive to the consumer. However, the number-one selling point for most consumers is the answer to the simple question, "How much?"

In the previous section, we discuss a cell phone contract versus a flat-rate monthly bill. Any consumer who purchases a cell phone understands that this is not a one-time bill. Cell phone bills are the gift that keeps on giving—month, after month, after month.

We asked consumers how much they paid for the convenience of a cell phone. You can see in Figure 9.4, the amount varies by age. The majority of consumers (55.1%) aged 55 and older are more conservative with their phone usage, paying $50 or less per month. When we look at the $51–100 monthly bill, 18–34 year-olds are the largest group (38.4%). Once you add a text plan, it is extremely easy to enter into the $100 range—trust me; I am talking from personal experience.

FIGURE 9.4: Cell Phone Bill (average per month)

	18–34	35–54	55+
$1-$50	30.9%	35.9%	55.1%
$51-$100	38.4%	31.1%	28.5%
$101-$150	19.5%	19.5%	9.9%
$150-$200	6.9%	9.0%	3.6%
$201 or more	4.3%	4.5%	2.8%

Source: BIGinsight.com

I am particularly amazed by consumers paying $201 or more for their phone bill—4.3% of 18–34 year olds are in this category. This consumer group must have (a) talked, texted, and used their phone non-stop, (b) make a lot of money and don't care about the phone bill, or (c) have the phone bill paid by someone else. This Figure confirms that I am a very frugal customer. I like my phone, but not for $200 a month—I barely like my phone for $100 a month.

Fickle friends

If I don't like a movie, I leave. If I don't like a party, I go home. If I don't like my cell phone service, I change phone company providers. Some people call me fickle. Others call me demanding. I simply think that a company should keep its promises. If they promise no dropped calls, the calls shouldn't be dropped. After talking to dead air, I decided it was time to switch cell phone providers.

In retailing, there is a saying that it is easier to keep a customer than to attract a new one. Having been in retailing since 1976, I can tell you that the saying is absolutely true. Furthermore, once you make a consumer angry, he or she is likely to tell absolutely everyone who will listen. I believe this, too, because in addition to working in the retailing industry I am a customer—I have some wild stories about really bad service.

Switching cell phone providers is not as easy as switching dry cleaners or grocers. Cell phone providers instill a very strong incentive to stay with the company—it is called a contract. If you break the contract, you are required to pay a penalty. The usual penalty is about $200. As Figure 9.5 demonstrates, this incentive works well. Consumers aged 18–34 are active switchers during 2010, with 16.1% saying goodbye. This is a large percentage; I suspect it would be larger without the contract. Meanwhile, consumers aged 35–54 also made their opinions very clear, with 9.9% saying so long. Even the 55 and older group switched providers. Clearly, consumers are willing to voice their opinions by changing providers.

FIGURE 9.5: SWITCHED CELL PHONE PROVIDERS

	18–34	35–54	55+
Yes	16.1%	9.9%	6.3%
No	83.9%	90.1%	93.7%

Source: BIGinsight.com

I want more from our relationship

Advanced technology makes cell phones comparable to mini-computers. Some phones allow users to access the Internet, play videos, games, music, photos, and keep them on track with GPS. The million-dollar question, however, is "What attributes are most important to consumers?"

FIGURE 9.6: CELL PHONE ATTRIBUTES DESIRED

	18–34	35–54	55+
Coverage	31.7%	27.1%	30.2%
Customer service	21.7%	19.2%	18.7%
Free minutes plan	19.0%	15.5%	13.7%
Handset variety	14.4%	7.8%	3.3%
Internet/Web access	28.2%	12.2%	10.1%
Music downloads	11.5%	3.6%	2.3%
Plan options	29.2%	22.2%	17.9%
Pricing/value	46.3%	53.0%	50.1%
Reliability (fewer dropped calls)	20.3%	16.0%	16.8%
Service	21.9%	17.2%	16.3%
Technology	16.3%	10.9%	7.5%
Text messaging plans	16.9%	15.4%	9.6%
Video services	4.3%	1.7%	0.9%
Other	6.5%	8.8%	18.7%

Source: BIGinsight.com

Regardless of age, three attributes are identified as the most important (Figure 9.6). Pricing and value are the most important by all age groups. The third most important attribute is coverage. Consumers care less about the fancy video capability than the price of the phone. The handset doesn't matter if the phone coverage is limited. No wonder Verizon's "Can you hear me now?" commercial is so successful.

You aren't the only one who wants me

Prior to the 1980s, the major landline phone company was nicknamed "Ma Bell." Ma Bell kept everyone in touch. The phone numbers started with the alphabet. My childhood phone number was Kenwood 59684. Consumers didn't have choices among phone providers. Ma Bell served everyone.

During the 1980s, Ma Bell deregulated and consumers were able to select a phone provider. With the advent of cell phone providers, the industry began to feel like the Wild West. Companies came on the scene and began promising everything and anything. Marketing efforts compared companies, products, services, and reputations. There was big money to be made and every company wanted the gold that was at the end of the rainbow—or at least as much of the cash as possible from as many of the customers as possible.

From the long list of cell phone providers on Figure 9.7, it is clear that consumers have many cell phone providers in which to choose. The four most popular cell phone providers are Verizon Wireless, AT&T Wireless, T-Mobile USA and Sprint Nextel. Verizon Wireless has the greatest percent of consumers (ranging from 29.8% to 33.8%). AT&T Wireless is the second most popular company (ranging from 25.2% to 27.3%). Sprint Nextel and T-Mobile USA are also popular but to a smaller extent. These companies attracted 18–54 year olds, however, only around 10%. Clearly, consumers are attracted to the Verizon Wireless or AT&T Wireless brands.

FIGURE 9.7: CELL PHONE PROVIDERS

	18–34	35–54	55+
Alltel Wireless	1.6%	0.9%	1.2%
AT&T Wireless	27.3%	25.2%	27.2%
Boost Mobile	1.8%	1.7%	0.3%
Cellular One	0.4%	0.1%	0.3%
Centennial Wireless	0.4%	0.1%	0.2%
Cincinnati Bell Wireless	0.5%	0.3%	0.4%
Cricket Communications	1.9%	1.9%	0.5%
Great Call/Jitterbug	0.2%	0.0%	0.1%
MetroPCS	2.7%	1.9%	0.4%
Revol Wireless	0.0%	0.2%	0.0%
Sprint Nextel	10.1%	10.7%	6.2%
Qwest Communications	0.1%	0.0%	0.0%
T-Mobile USA	11.9%	9.4%	8.3%
TracFone	3.6%	8.0%	10.9%
U.S. Cellular	2.4%	2.6%	1.9%
Verizon Wireless	29.8%	30.1%	33.8%
Virgin Mobile	2.4%	2.5%	2.3%
Wal-Mart Family Mobile	0.4%	0.3%	0.1%
Other	2.6%	4.0%	5.6%

Source: BIGinsight.com

My mom calls me smart for a reason

Names are important. The Big Mac brings to mind a really big sandwich. Ralph Lauren Polo evokes equestrian elegance. "Man cave" conjures up a safe haven for men watching sports, drinking beer, and sitting with your feet on the furniture without worrying about being rebuked. When it came time to name a phone that "does it all," the only possible one was *smartphone*. A smartphone is the generic term for a phone that allows the user to access the Internet, download applications (known as apps), access e-mail, and, of course, make phone calls and send text messages. So who needs a smartphone? Is it only for smart people?

Take a look at Figure 9.8. Consumers have definite purchasing behaviors regarding smartphones. Consumers aged 18–34 are the frontrunners for having purchased a smart phone (48.6%). Just take a look on any high school or college campus. They all seem to have and "need" a smartphone. Perhaps it will help them earn better grades in school?

Consumers aged 35-54 aren't as impressed with the technology. Only 30.4% possess a smartphone. But this looks like a lot when compared with consumers 55 years or older — only 15.1% of this group has a smartphone. Age really does matter when adopting new technology from your cell phone carrier.

FIGURE 9.8: SMARTPHONE OWNERS

	18–34	35–54	55+
Yes	48.6%	30.4%	15.1%
No	51.4%	69.6%	84.9%

Source: BIGinsight.com

Who says I'm needy?

Cell phone providers entice consumers by showing them additional attributes. They first attract you with an introductory price. Once you sign the contract, they encourage you to look at all the "shiny new phone attributes" for your next phone. It can absolutely be addictive. Who knew I couldn't live without a combination cell phone/calendar/calculator/address book. Perhaps I'm just needy?

FIGURE 9.9: CELL PHONE ATTRIBUTES

	18–34	35–54	55+
Address book	44.5%	45.6%	45.3%
Bluetooth	37.8%	41.8%	34.7%
Calculator	49.4%	44.0%	34.1%
Calendar	48.0%	45.8%	38.2%
Caller ID	55.6%	64.5%	66.1%
Call forwarding	31.3%	29.4%	27.2%
Camera-enabled	53.1%	62.2%	59.5%
Choice of phone color	33.4%	27.8%	24.0%
Color screen	48.0%	45.4%	36.5%
Downloadable ringtones	32.8%	33.4%	27.1%
Downloadable screensavers	24.3%	22.6%	15.9%
E-mail access	48.3%	52.5%	42.5%
Flip phone	15.0%	19.0%	26.3%
Games	38.4%	25.5%	11.3%
GSM capable	16.1%	13.8%	8.4%
Integrated PDA	18.1%	15.9%	11.3%
Internet/Web access	49.2%	50.9%	38.1%
Meeting planner	15.5%	13.1%	4.8%
Mobile TV	21.4%	16.5%	5.3%
Music downloads	28.6%	24.1%	10.7%
Navigation/GPS	36.8%	34.3%	31.3%
One-touch dialing (speed dialing)	27.4%	27.5%	33.9%
Push-to-talk or walkie-talkie-enabled	12.4%	11.0%	5.0%
Speaker phone	48.1%	53.5%	49.1%
Streaming video	29.3%	20.7%	10.6%
Text messaging	60.0%	63.0%	47.6%
Three-way calling	28.6%	26.6%	18.5%
Voice-activated dialing	23.9%	27.7%	25.9%
Voicemail	44.0%	53.0%	48.0%
Other	3.1%	3.7%	5.9%

Source: BIGinsight.com

We asked consumers which attributes they looked for in a cell phone. Understanding that consumers "want it all"—and that's okay—we examined where 50% or more of consumers in each age bracket identified the desired attribute (Refer to Figure 9.9). These include caller ID, camera-enabled, and text messaging. One caveat is given to the text messaging attribute: Only 47.6% of persons aged 55 and older desire this attribute. However, a whopping 60% of 18–34 and 63% of 35–54 year-olds desire text messaging. As such, it is included in the group. Personally, I would have thought voice mail is more important than being camera-enabled.

Tweet-tweet

Tweeting—or using Twitter—has its advantages and disadvantages. One advantage is that you are only allowed 140 characters per post. This requires the user to think very carefully about what he or she is going to say. Unlike e-mail, where you can post a long diatribe, a tweet needs to be short and sweet. The somewhat unusual concept of Twitter is that, for the most part, people who tweet talk about nothing. In that way, Twitter is a lot like the idea behind *Seinfeld*—a show about nothing. For example, Jane tweets, "I'm at Starbucks." Twelve of her nearest and dearest friends tweet back saying, "Cool."

Of course, if you are a celebrity, tweeting is a way to keep in contact with fans. Stephen Fry (comedian and actor), Lance Armstrong (athlete), Britney Spears (singer), Rick Sanchez (news anchor), Shaquille O'Neill (athlete), and John Cleese (comedian and actor) are the top six celebrity tweeters. Perhaps consumers who like the tweets feel as if they are being "touched by royalty" (Ahmed, 2009).

Figure 9.10 shows the most active tweeters by age; 12.7% of the 18–34 year olds tweet regularly. Only 5.3% of 35–54 year olds tweet regularly. Consumers 55 years and older are really "out of tweet" (1.9%). This is a young person's way to communicate.

FIGURE 9.10: FREQUENCY OF TWITTER USAGE

	18–34	35–54	55+
Regularly	12.7%	5.3%	1.9%
Occasionally	19.8%	14.7%	8.7%
Never	67.5%	80.1%	89.4%

Source: BIGinsight.com

My 1,500 closest friends

In 1984, AT&T featured a commercial with the tagline "Reach out and touch someone." You should be able to watch the commercial by visiting YouTube (and more about YouTube later). Unbeknown to AT&T, Mark Zuckerberg, creator of Facebook, would devise a social media platform that allowed consumers to do just that—reach out and touch (or at least poke) someone.

No one can deny that Facebook has changed the way consumers communicate with one another. Facebook made finding long-lost friends, posting photos (the good, the bad, and the downright tragic) for the world to see, and blending your professional and casual worlds so much easier. Facebook opened up lines of communication. This communication can be positive and negative. Companies use Facebook to promote sales, events, and their brands. Employees sometimes cross the professional line by ranting and raving about bad bosses, less than ideal work environments, or employee "relationships." College students post photos of themselves in all manner of inebriation, forgetting that prospective employers can and will find the photos.

Facebook—for all its wonderful attributes—places consumers on a very open platform. As Kramer from *Seinfeld* said, "I'm out there, Jerry, and I'm loving every minute of it!" What percent of consumers who were surveyed are "out there"? Of consumers' aged 18–34, 65.2% are regular users of Facebook, while 46.7% of those aged 35–54 also use the site regularly (Figure 9.11). As consumers aged, their use of social media declined, with only 24.2% of those aged 55 and older using Facebook regularly.

FIGURE 9.11: FACEBOOK USAGE BY AGE

	18–34	35–54	55+
Regularly	65.2%	46.7%	24.2%
Occasionally	20.2%	25.7%	31.8%
Never	14.7%	27.6%	44.0%

Source: BIGinsight.com

Reasons to use Facebook

The reasons for creating a personal Facebook page or logging on to someone else's are numerous. They range from communication (for example, to chat), personal gain (you could try to win a contest), entertainment (playing games), and hedonic (such as a display of personal achievements) to business (to highlight business features). We asked consumers to list the reasons why they use Facebook (see Figure 9.12). The data reveals the changing nature of how our society socializes and markets products. Consumers use Facebook for coupons, sweepstakes and free offers. The marketing appeal to young groups could bring in large numbers of consumers. Likewise, consumers use Facebook as a socialization tool. Facebook can be used to "humanize" a retail business. Through strategic messages and images, business are able to build their brand in the consumer's mind using Facebook.

FIGURE 9.12: Reasons Consumers Use Facebook (Sampling of Verbatim Responses)

Entertainment

- Blow my kids' minds
- Games
- Contests
- Coupons and free offers
- Giveaways, sweepstakes
- A way to entertain myself and pass time
- Read stuff re products, TV shows
- Send Facebook mail

Conformity

- Because everyone else does

Socialize

- Share opinions
- Socialize
- Stay connected with friends and family
- Stay in contact with long-distance friends
- To be polite when asked to be a "friend"
- Just [to] keep in touch
- Just to stay relevant
- Just to view my friends' walls
- See what friends are doing
- Just to view my friends' walls

Business

- Advertise for business
- As a networking tool
- Business promotion
- Networking for jobs

Family

- Because family wanted me to use
- Post videos and pictures of my family
- Catch up [on] what family members are up to
- Chat online with family and friends

Source: BIGinsight.com

TXT me :-)

Texting—or sending messages via a cell phone using a combination of words, numbers, and symbols—is a relatively new form of communication. Texting only became popular between 2001 and 2004 as the technology advanced. Texting enables the user to send messages discreetly and without using valuable cell phone minutes. For example, consumers can communicate via texting while in a movie theatre or during a lecture. Although this drives me crazy (pun intended), I've seen people driving their car on the freeway while simultaneously texting. Needless to say, I move to a different lane as quickly as possible.

We asked consumers to list their reasons for texting. Consumers' text for a wide variety of reasons; reasons range from the mundane (for example, what's for dinner?) to the critical (where are the kids?) to the very important (such as how to have fun). Glance at the categories on Figure 9.13. Identify the number of items that are similar to your text list. The three main reasons for texting are keeping in touch with family and friends, answering a quick business message or confirming an appointment. Texting helps consumers stay connected and organized.

FIGURE 9.13: REASONS FOR TEXTING (SAMPLING OF VERBATIM RESPONSES)

Family & Friends

- Family matters
- Family commitments
- Family schedules, questions
- Finding relatives
- Family matters
- Family commitments
- School, events, gossip
- Social events
- TV shows, people's problems, work, plans for later

- Wellbeing of family and friends
- Working late or getting groceries
- Getting together with friends
- Gossip
- Family schedules, questions
- Finding relatives
- Family matters
- Family commitments
- Catching up with friends
- Catching up with my kids
- Chatting with friends
- Check on kids, everyday happenings, when and where I am going
- Course of the day's events
- Communicate with family that way
- Communication with my spouse
- Family schedules, questions
- Finding relatives
- Asking when family will be home, dinner ready, that kind of thing
- Bits of interesting information with family and friends

Business

- Answer a text
- Asking quick questions that do not require a phone call
- Confirming appointments/time
- Customer contact
- A quick message
- Absolutely important issues
- If I am running late, or something that only needs one response
- Important updates if unable to reach a person

Schedule/Logistics

- Appointments
- Asking people to call me when I'm not sure they can answer the phone
- Current events, life happenings, whereabouts
- Daily plans
- Dated events
- Dinner, where to go, who to see
- Directions

Source: BIGinsight.com

You won't believe this?!

YouTube is the ultimate social media platform for voyeurs and exhibitionists. You may think that this statement is a bit out of line, but think about the main principle of YouTube. YouTube allows people to videotape themselves and share their videos with millions of viewers worldwide.

Some of the videos shown on YouTube are cute home movies. Other videos portray wild and wacky stunts that may or may not be altered using technology. Still others highlight media sensations such as Susan Boyle's singing debut. Regardless of the type of video, no one can deny that thousands of people regularly watch YouTube videos.

We asked consumers how much they used YouTube. As revealed in Figure 9.14, consumers aged 18–34 years old regularly use the website (51.2%). As a college professor, I can attest to the popularity of YouTube among this age group. Each week, students inform me of another "must see" YouTube video.

Consumers aged 35–54 aren't as active with the YouTube videos; 52.6% occasionally using YouTube and only 24.6% regularly visit the site. As consumers age, the use of YouTube declines significantly. Only 10% of consumers aged 55 and older use YouTube regularly. I must admit, however, I have a friend in this age bracket. He sends me YouTube videos at least once every other week. Although he doesn't admit it, I suspect he is on YouTube every day. The interesting fact about this friend is he is a VP at a large company. When I asked him about his using YouTube, he said, "I like to know everything."

FIGURE 9.14: YouTube Usage by Age

	18-34	35-54	55+
Regularly	51.2%	24.6%	10.0%
Occasionally	39.1%	52.6%	46.3%
Never	9.7%	22.8%	43.7%

Source: BIGinsight.com

Summary

For anyone who has ever felt alone, cell phone providers and the Internet can help us feel connected to the world. Just by a click, keystroke, or acceptance to a friend request on Facebook, we can meet up with thousands of people who are instantly our newest BFFs.

Younger consumers readily adopt the use of Facebook and text messaging. Socialization is the number 1 reason consumer use Facebook and text messaging. The technology allows users to build virtual relationships, share stories and expand their world beyond their immediate community.

Top five lessons learned

1. The three top reasons consumers 55 and older switch cell phone providers are: (a) coverage, (b) price, and (c) customer service.

2. The three most important attributes in a cell phone differ by age. In other words, cell phone providers would be wise to market phone attributes (such as text messaging, camera-enabled, or caller ID capabilities) based on the age of the target market.

3. Twitter is popular among stars as a promotional tool, but not heavily adopted by the majority of consumers.

4. The majority of Facebook users are aged 18–34 years old.

5. Consumers text family and friends about everything!

References

Ahmed, M. "The 50 Most Popular Celebs on Twitter." *Sunday Times* (2009) Retrieved February 25, 2011 from http://technology.timesonline.co.uk/tol/ news/tech_and_web/article5641893.ece

Chapter

10

The Washington Trifecta:
Politics, National Security, and Taxes

There are three concepts that bind all Americans together: politics, national security, and taxes. They bind together like superglue. Have you ever put superglue on your finger by mistake? If not, you are lucky. Superglue on any surface, including human skin, will bond to another surface almost immediately. Superglue is *fabulous* for bonding, binding, and adhering contact surfaces together—unless you accidently bond your finger to the table.

Many consumers' perceptions, opinions, and perspectives toward politics, the nation's security, and taxes are like superglue. Once hardened, rarely are they pulled apart, changed, or altered. Think about it. When was the last time you dramatically changed your opinion about the IRS? Do you know of any political activists? Can you imagine them telling you they don't plan on voting?

X marks the spot

Right or left, good or bad, vocal or silent, most consumers have definitive opinions regarding politics, national security, and taxes. These opinions influence the fabric of our nation. It would be naïve to write a book on the changing trends of America without examining this subject.

In recent years, elected officials regardless of party affiliation emphasize the importance of voting. Voting is a part of our national constitution and foundation of our freedom. In June 2010, we surveyed consumers across the United States, asking them if they are registered voters. We then segmented them into two groups: consumers living in households earning $50,000 or more; and all consumer households regardless of income (Figure 10.1). In our sample, 88.3% of consumers in households earning $50,000 or more are registered voters. The percent of all consumers who are registered voters is equally impressive at 83.3%. Regardless of income, the majority of consumers are registered to vote.

FIGURE 10.1: REGISTERED VOTERS – JUNE 2010

Are you a registered voter?	$50K+	All
Yes	88.3%	83.3%
No, but I plan to register before the November 2010 midterm congressional elections	3.7%	5.4%
No	8.0%	11.2%

Source: BIGinsight.com

My opinion matters

Not all registered voters make it to the polls on Election Day. In the 2004 presidential election, 64% of the eligible voters marched to the polls. At the time, this was an historic all-time high for citizens voicing their opinions on who should be their president (Holder, 2006).

During 2008, an initiative called "Get out the vote" was undertaken to in an effort to increase voter turnout. Political advertisements frequently reminded consumers of the importance of political affiliation, party lines, and the power of the vote.

In June 2010, consumers were asked if they planned to vote in the November 2008 midterm congressional election. Figure 10.2 reveals that approximately three-fourths of the sample, regardless of income, planned to vote in the election. A variety of words to express the phenomenon that occurred in 2008 may include change, hope, or optimism; regardless of the word, citizens went in droves to the polls with the belief that their opinion mattered.

FIGURE 10.2: PLAN TO VOTE IN NOVEMBER 2008 MIDTERM CONGRESSIONAL ELECTION

	$50K+	All
Yes	77.9%	72.4%
No	7.9%	9.0%
Undecided	14.1%	18.6%

Source: BIGinsight.com

History in the making

The 2008 presidential campaign electrified the nation. The results had the potential for making historic firsts in the nation. If Obama won the election, he would be the first African-American president. If McCain won the election, he would bring with him the first female vice president. The two men and their campaigns fought week after week, month after month for the most powerful job in the world. Consumers flocked to the polls. Over 91% of consumers in households of $50,000 or more voted. All consumers were almost as patriotic, with 86.8% voting in the 2008 presidential election (Figure 10.3). The world knows by now that history was made when the election polls closed. Historic numbers of voters turned out at the polls and the first African-American president was elected to office.

FIGURE 10.3: VOTED IN 2008 PRESIDENTIAL ELECTION

	$50K+	All
Yes	91.5%	86.8%
No	8.5%	13.2%

Source: BIGinsight.com

Déjà vu?

Washington has a very exclusive club. As of 2011, only forty-four men have been admitted to the club. The club is called president of the United States. Requirements for the club include fierce ambition, stamina, charisma, and a passion for serving the people. Once a person becomes a member of the club, he typically desires to be an *active* member for eight years. Once designated as a member, his recognition is maintained for life.

Let's be honest—or at least realistic—those who get elected to the highest office in the land don't necessarily need to be the smartest person in the room. He (or maybe sometime in the future she) need not be the best senator, governor, or community leader. Charisma, the ability to communicate, and inspire the nation are three of the most important characteristics.

President Obama is charismatic and has the ability to communicate. His message of change and hope during his campaign drove millions of voters to the polls. Under Obama's tenure (although not necessarily because of his tenure), the country suffers with the most difficult economic times since the Great Depression of the 1930s. Unemployment is high, the stock market fluctuates, and consumers protest on Wall Street. Under the circumstances any sitting elected official probably wonders "If the election is held today, would I win?

In January 2011, we asked consumers "If the election were held today, would they vote for President Obama." As shown in Figure 10.4 if an election had been held in 2011, there could well have been a new member in the club: 38.5% stated that they would vote for someone other than Obama; an additional 28.5% were undecided; while only 33.1% backed the President. Only time will tell if President Obama will have a second term. Citizens have a lot of time to change their minds between now and the next election.

FIGURE 10.4: PRESIDENTIAL ELECTIONS RESULTS

	All
President Obama	33.1%
Someone else	38.5%
Undecided	28.5%

Source: BIGinsight.com

Let's party!

Political party affiliation has a tendency to be a source of division among consumers, business persons, and politicians. The 2008 presidential race brought out some dramatic grievances. Joe Lieberman, a lifelong Democrat who had won his Senate seat in 2006 as an "Independent Democrat" came out in open support for the Republican McCain. This change also signaled to the Democrat senators that they could not automatically count on his vote. Times were indeed changing.

We asked consumers to indicate their party affiliation. Consumers are segmented into two groups: consumers in households of $50,000 or more; and all consumers. As we look at the consumers in households earning $50,000 or more, party affiliation reveal perhaps the changing times associated with politics (Figure 10.5). The two largest political affiliations, Democrats (39.2%) and Republicans (33.4%), are expected. The relatively large percent of Independent voters (22%) is particularly interesting. This group is based on the political platform. The remaining two groups, Libertarian (1.5%) and Other (4%), are relatively small.

The examination of consumers' party affiliation is interesting. Similar to consumers in households of $50,000+, Democrats (40.6%) and Republicans (30.5%) are the largest political affiliations. With 22.3% declaring themselves as Independent, they echo consumers in the higher income bracket. The remaining two groups, Libertarian (1.5%) and other (5%), are also relatively small.

Income is often touted as an indicator of political party affiliation. The Democrat party is often viewed as being (a) for the working class, (b) understanding of union laborers, and (c) representative of minorities. The Republican party is often viewed as being (a) for wealthy consumers, (b) understanding of Wall Street, and (c) full of socialites.

FIGURE 10.5: POLITICAL PARTY

	$50K+	All
Republican	33.4%	30.5%
Democrat	39.2%	40.6%
Libertarian	1.5%	1.5%
Independent	22.0%	22.3%
Other	4.0%	5.0%

Source: BIGinsight.com

Results of our survey reveal that income does not necessarily indicate a consumer's propensity toward a political party. As we look at the two columns, the small differences between the two groups are evident. However, if income were a key predictor, there should be a larger gap between Republican and Democrat based on income.

An interesting point is that the Independent party is also represented by a healthy proportion in each income group; 22.0% of consumers earning $50,000+ and 22.3% of all consumers. The Independent party may consist of consumers voting across party lines as opposed to straight ticket.

Are we safe?

National security tends to be part of the platform on many political campaigns. Since 9/11, consumers' sense of safety continues to be a hot-button topic. Abandoned cars in New York streets are cause to call out the bomb squad. Suspicious white powder mailed to news rooms result in the FBI being called.

With all of these dramatic changes in our lives, we asked consumers to identify their level of confidence in the nation's security. Look at Figure 10.6. In June 2003, 29.3% are confident or very confident of the nation's security. Year after year, their confidence is slowly deteriorating. In 2007, a slight increase is seen; perhaps consumers see a glimmer of hope. But just one year later, confidence dips to all time low. In June 2010, only 19.2% of the consumers surveyed are confident in the nation's security.

The U.S. is safer than many countries — Egypt, Palestine, and Afghanistan, for example. However when 80.8% of the consumers surveyed in June 2010 are feeling neutral or not confident about the nation's security, there is a problem. Or at least *they* perceive a problem.

FIGURE 10.6: LEVEL OF CONFIDENCE IN THE NATION'S SECURITY

	Jun-03	Jun-04	Jun-05	Jun-06	Jun-07	Jun-08	Jun-09	Jun-10
Very confident	3.7%	6.5%	5.7%	2.8%	5.5%	3.2%	3.4%	3.2%
Confident	25.6%	22.8%	27.4%	19.7%	30.6%	11.9%	16.8%	16.0%

Source: BIGinsight.com

Death and taxes

People can rely on two events: death and taxes. Of course, there are plenty of people who try to avoid paying their taxes. Many of them end up in colorful orange jumpsuits and guests of the state for three to five years. *And* they also are required to pay the back taxes plus a penalty. Let's face it: It's just easier to accept that taxes are a way of life and pay the IRS. Besides, taxes are a topic of national conversation among politicians, business persons, and consumers. Comedians use the topic during their late-night routines, while politicians use it to gain voter support. You can't live with taxes and you can't live without taxes.

We asked consumers to indicate how they will prepare their 2011 taxes. We segmented consumers into two groups: consumers in households of $50,000 or more; and all consumers. Take a look at Figure 10.7. Two distinct trends are revealed. The prominent use of computer software to complete taxes is the first trend. More than one-third of consumers in households earning $50,000 or more and among all consumers used programs such as Quicken or TurboTax. The steep decline in consumers preparing the taxes by hand is the second trend. Instead, consumers, regardless of income, are using an accountant or tax specialist.

FIGURE 10.7: METHODS OF TAX PREPARATION

	$50K+	All
Prepare myself by hand	8.7%	10.1%
Prepare myself using computer software	43.9%	39.7%
Use an accountant	23.4%	19.3%
Use a tax preparation service	14.9%	20.9%
Have spouse, friend, or other relative prepare	9.1%	10.1%

Source: BIGinsight.com

Snail mail or e-file?

Technology is wonderful. It makes the processing of information go fast – very fast. The IRS uses technology to process billions of tax forms faster and more efficiently. This means that consumers are able to get their refund back in a few weeks instead of a few months. Of course, not everyone likes, uses, or understands technology. Personally, if it meant I receive a refund faster, I will learn the technology as fast as I can, or hire a CPA.

We asked consumers if they planned to file online. Look at Figure 10-8. Approximately 69% of consumers earning $50,000 or more plan to file online compared with 65% of all consumers. The benefit of online filing is obvious: obtaining the refund fast. So why would consumers avoid filing electronically? Consumers who don't file online may (a) owe money and write a check, (b) not trust the electronic filing system, or (c) not want sensitive information sent over the Internet. In the near future, it is expected that nearly all consumer taxes will be filed online. No postage required!

FIGURE 10.8: FILE TAXES ONLINE

	$50K+	All
Yes	69.0%	65.0%
No	31.0%	35.0%

Source: BIGinsight.com

Tax sale!

Tax season is traditionally a well-known time for using extra cash for expenses. Retailers often have "tax refund sales" in an attempt to stimulate purchases, particularly big-ticket items. We inquired how they planned to spend their refund check. (Note that the respondents were able to indicate more than one answer, so the figures add up to more than 100%).

Figure 10.9 reveals that 48.1% of consumers earning $50,000 or more save some of the refund check. Paying down debt is the second largest use of the refund, with 45.4%. It is surprising to see that one fourth of the group (25.5%) plan to use the refund check on everyday expenses. This may suggest that consumers earning $50,000 or more are unable to meet their everyday expenses. The last two areas of spending using the refund check are major purchases (14.5%) and a vacation (15.9%). It is in these areas that retailers concentrate the heaviest amount of advertising to entice consumers to spend their tax refund.

The spending patterns of all consumers are similar to those consumers in the over $50,000 income bracket. Consumers mainly plan to pay down debt (46%), while placing a portion of the refund in savings is the second largest response (43.8%). Everyday expenses will be paid using tax refunds by 31.9% of the customers. The final two categories, major purchases (15.2%) and vacations (13.1%), are comparable responses to those of the higher-income consumers.

As the recession lingers along paying down debt and increasing savings continue to be all-important activities. This is definitely a different set of priorities than in the "spend as much as you can" 1980s. Consumers are learning to look toward the future rather than spending wildly on immediate gratification.

FIGURE 10.9: SPEND TAX REFUND CHECK

	$50K+	All
Pay down debt	45.4%	46.0%
Savings	48.1%	43.8%
Everyday expenses	25.5%	31.9%
Major purchase (TV, furniture, car, etc.)	14.5%	15.2%
Vacation	15.9%	13.1%

Source: BIGinsight.com

Summary

Being president of the United States is one of the most difficult jobs in the world. Just look at photos of each president and you can see how rapidly they age while in office. The hair turns gray, the dark circles becomes charcoal black, and the expensive suits cannot hide the weariness from lack of sleep and deep concern for the country.

Consumers typically have an opinion regarding how the country is being run. Consumers believe the country was no longer a safe haven; they no longer have positive feelings regarding their level of safety. Gone are the good old days—if they really existed, perhaps that was a myth.

Taxes are paid online and by snail mail. The IRS may be strongly encouraging consumers to file online, but some consumers still want to send the returns through the mail. Decreasing debt and increasing the savings accounts are the two most popular uses for tax refunds.

Top five lessons learned

1. More than 3/4th of the consumers surveyed are registered voters.

2. If the presidential election were held today, 38.5% would vote for someone other than President Obama.

3. Approximately 22% of all consumers and consumers earning $50,000 household income or more declare themselves as independents.

4. The majority of consumers surveyed are not confident about the nation's security.

5. The vast majority of consumers spend their tax refund by paying down debt or placing their money in savings.

References

Holder, K. "Population Characteristics." *Voting and Registration in the Election of November 2004* (March 2006) 20–556. Retrieved February 22, 2011 from http://www.census.gov/prod/2006pubs/p20-556.pdf

Malkin, M. "Paul Sperry: Another Spying Scandal at Gitmo." *New York Post* (December 1, 2009) Retrieved February 21, 2011 from http://michellemalkin.com/2009/12/01/paul-sperry-another -spying-scandal-at-gitmo/

Chapter

11

Things Aren't Working Out
as Planned

There's a song at the beginning of *Fiddler on the Roof* that expresses the importance of having a set of customs or beliefs that are passed from generation to generation, it's called simply *Tradition*. Traditions are wonderful. They make sense out of the world. Traditions give the illusion that our lives are stable. When I was young and naïve I identified several traditions that I thought were unshakeable. These traditions made America great. They were as follows:

1. Children would grow up to be more prosperous than their parents.

2. Our nation's leaders were to be admired, respected, and revered.

3. Our government could protect us from all harm.

The 1980s was the high point of these traditions. Consumers experienced a feeling of unending economic growth and excess. Nothing could stop the economy, the spending, or the joy of living. Or so many consumers and businesses believed. Then came 9/11. And then the economic collapse of 2008. The three traditions that I believed in have been shaken to the core. Across the nation, new, more humble traditions were being formed.

When will it end?

The recession that began in 2008 rocked the nation. Bankruptcies, foreclosures, unemployment, and pink slips made headline news every day. The only news was gloomy news. The 1980s days of excess were a distant memory. Consumers who had a flush bank account were cautious about spending money on luxury products — conspicuous consumption definitely was not in vogue. Consumers now focused on living within their means, purchasing with cash, and building a savings account.

As the economy moved along at a glacial pace, everyone had an opinion regarding the recession. News networks had time slots to fill, economists had charts and tables, and elected officials were concerned about their constituents and their jobs. The recession transformed the television talking heads into 24/7 news-entertainment shows. No one could agree about the status of the recession or how to fix the economy. Meanwhile, the number of foreclosed houses increased, unemployment grew, and consumers' frustrations grew.

In June 2009, the National Bureau of Economic Research declared the end of the recession. In case you missed this announcement or didn't realize that the economy was "back to normal," look at Figure 11.1. We asked over 5,000 consumers nationwide who they believed could determine when a recession has ended. An overwhelming majority of consumers (71.1%) believed that the American people, or consumers, (not politicians or economists) were in the best position to determine when a recession has ended. The second most popular answer was the economists with 15.9%.

FIGURE 11.1: DECIDING THE END OF THE RECESSION

Economists	15.9%
The President	6.0%
Congress	1.6%
American people/consumers	71.1%
Congressional Budget Office (CBO)	1.8%
Other	3.6%

Source: BIGinsight.com

We also asked consumers if they thought the recession was over. In September 2010, the answer was emphatic: 80.9% stated that the recession was not over — even though it had been declared so (Figure 11.2). Apparently, our national survey of consumers knows something the National Bureau of Economic Research doesn't.

FIGURE 11.2: THE END OF THE RECESSION

Is the recession over?	
Yes	9.3%
No	80.9%
I don't know	9.9%

Source: BIGinsight.com

As you look at Figure 11.3, you will soon understand what the National Bureau of Economic Research might have overlooked. We asked our respondents if their wealth had declined and if so, how? The sad but all too familiar results of the survey reveal that consumers' wealth continues to suffer as a result of multiple factors. 46.8% of the consumers indicate that their home values are dropping; 40.1% are affected by lost jobs. Stock market investments decline with 38.2% of consumers. Consumers are being pounded financially from the right and left. They simply can't catch a break; no wonder 80.9% believe the recession marches on.

FIGURE 11.3: HOW WEALTH HAS DECLINED

Investment in stock market declined	38.2%
Value of home declined	46.8%
Interest rates on savings declined	38.2%
Lost job	40.1%
Real estate investments declined	13.2%
Other	12.0%

Source: BIGinsight.com

The sign of a real economic recovery is when consumers start spending similarly to prior to the recession. Three-fourths (77.1%) of the consumers surveyed stated that they are not ready to start spending again as they did prior to the recession (Figure 11.4). Perhaps the average consumer never will spend like that again. Perhaps a more responsible spending pattern, a more cautious debt-free spending pattern, is in their future. Only time will tell.

FIGURE 11.4: SPENDING PATTERNS PRIOR TO THE RECESSION

Ready to start spending again as prior to recession ...	
Yes	22.9%
No	77.1%

Source: BIGinsight.com

Tell me how you really feel

When I was a little kid, my grade school teacher told me that every man could grow up to be president. Her statement was made in reverence and awe for the person holding the office. Nowadays, we might think that my teacher was a bit old-fashioned using the word "man," but facts are facts. Forty years later, no woman has entered the hallowed halls of the White House as president.

The president of the United States needs a very thick skin. Consumers, politicians, newscasters, columnists, voters, non-voters all have an opinion on the president's every move. Is he doing enough for the economy? Why did he play golf on the day the market went down? Why did his wife, family, and forty of their closest friends go to Spain during the country's worst economic crisis since the 1930s? During the campaign and while in office, the president and his family live in a fishbowl—granted, it is a very luxurious fishbowl.

In September 2010, we asked a random sample of consumers to state their overall opinion of President Obama's job in one word. The results are segmented into positive and negative (Figure 11.5). Overall, 20.9% are positive about the president's efforts. They believe he is *trying, confident, fair,* and *positive.* The "negative" group (13.2%) is less forgiving of President Obama's efforts. They view his efforts as a *failure, ineffective, bad, poor,* and *terrible.* (Note that 64% indicate "unsure," "other," or did not provide a response.)

History will show that regardless of who holds the title of president, one hundred percent of his (or her) constituents will not agree with the results, efforts, or policies being put forward. In the meantime, news networks, politicians, and consumers will voice their opinions. The ability to voice our opinions is what makes America great.

FIGURE 11.5: OPINION REGARDING THE PRESIDENT'S EFFORTS

Positive		Negative	
Good	5.8%	Disappointed	2.5%
Okay	4.4%	Bad	2.2%
Trying	3.4%	Poor	1.5%
Hopeful	2.4%	Sucks	1.4%
Great	2.2%	Incompetent	1.2%
Confident	1.1%	Socialist	1.2%
Fair	0.9%	Liar	1.0%
Positive	0.7%	Failure	0.8%
		Disgusted	0.8%
		Ineffective	0.8%
		Terrible	0.8%
Subtotal	20.9%	Subtotal	13.2%

Source: BIGinsight.com

Using the same categories (positive, negative), we asked consumers to also state in one word their opinion about Congress. Check out Figure 11.6. Only 5.5% of those sampled perceive Congress as doing an acceptable job. The strongest positive word used is *good*. This definitely isn't high praise, but at least it is positive. *Okay* and *fair* are the other two descriptors of Congress. These are definitely not glowing words of praise, but our elected representatives should take what they can get, since almost one-fourth (24.8%) of those surveyed have very definitive and negative opinions regarding Congress. Examples of terms used to describe those on the Hill include *terrible, sucks, disgusted, corrupt, greedy, failure, incompetent,* and *ineffective.* Ouch, these are very strong words; particularly considering these are our elected officials. (Again, note that 64% indicated "other" or did not provide a response.)

FIGURE 11.6: OPINIONS REGARDING CONGRESS

Positive		Negative	
Okay	2.9%	Bad	4.2%
Good	1.7%	Sucks	2.8%
Fair	0.9%	Disappointed	2.4%
		Poor	2.3%
		Terrible	1.7%
		Disgusted	1.5%
		Useless	1.5%
		Stupid	1.4%
		Corrupt	1.2%
		Greedy	1.0%
		Failure	1.0%
		Frustrated	1.0%
		Incompetent	1.0%
		Ineffective	1.0%
		Sad	0.8%
		Selfish	0.8%
		Lousy	0.8%
Subtotal	5.5%	Subtotal	24.8%

Source: BIGinsight.com

How could you be so dumb to send that through e-mail?

The Internet and all that goes with it (such as e-mail and social media) allows consumers to interact with lightning speed. Friends, neighbors, and even strangers across the nation and internationally can learn about your daily activities, daughter's dance recital, or the latest gossip from the office.

When you were in grade school, you probably learned that it wasn't polite to "gossip" about other people. The Internet and social media dilutes this lesson. E-mail, Facebook, and YouTube are being used by a great number of people to rant, vent, and gossip.

In addition to being unprofessional, this behavior can have long-lasting negative effects. Just in case you have forgotten or were vacationing when the WikiLeaks affair began, let's recap. Julian Assange is the founder of an organization called WikiLeaks. Assange believes that it is important to find out and expose companies' secrets. In 2010, Assange's organization obtained millions of confidential U.S. diplomatic cables. The U.S. government stated that if Assange and his organization released the cables, lives would be in danger (Alberts, 2010). Meanwhile, some of the cables included less than flattering comments on world leaders. Secretary of State Clinton went into overdrive trying to mend international fences (Leonard & Burns, 2010).

Confidential information is obviously meant for only those parties intended to know the information. However, unflattering information was sent via a cable. Who is responsible for this correspondence? Is the person who wrote and sent the cable responsible? Or perhaps those responsible are the ones who found and distributed the information?

We asked consumers nationwide who is to blame for WikiLeaks—and in particular for placing the unflattering information in writing. Take a look at Figure 11.7. A whopping 61% believe that Julian Assange *and* the U.S. government are responsible. Only 19.3% of the sample solely blame Assange. It goes to show, when there is gossip being spread around, most people believe two parties are involved and should be held accountable.

FIGURE 11.7: RESPONSIBILITY FOR WIKILEAKS

Julian Assange	19.3%
Government officials	13.4%
Both	61.0%
Neither	6.3%

Source: BIGinsight.com

Flying the friendly skies

After the 9/11 tragedy, consumers expanded their vocabulary: Transportation Security Administration (TSA). The TSA is designed to make the U.S. airports secure from terrorists. Banned items on flights include: liquids larger than three ounces, guns, and sharp items such as penknives. The TSA makes flying the skies safe.

If you travel a lot, you know that the TSA is not without controversy. Is the cost worth the risk? Are the methods effective? How are the individuals trained? We decided to ask consumers their overall opinion of the TSA. Figure 11.8 shows consumers opinions of the TSA's level of effectiveness in stopping terrorism. In March 2011, 39.7% agreed that the TSA is doing an effective job in stopping terrorists. Of course, as with opinions regarding the effectiveness of the president and Congress, not everyone feels the same way: 27.8% believes TSA is not effective in stopping terrorists; and 32.4% are neutral.

FIGURE 11.8: TSA is Effective in Stopping Terrorism

1–2 Strongly disagree to disagree	27.8%
3 Neither agree nor disagree	32.4%
4–5 Somewhat agree to agree	39.7%
Average	3.1

Source: BIGinsight.com

Now take a look at Figure 11.9. We asked if the TSA is worth the hassle; 42.7% believe the long lines, body scans, and check-in counters are worth the hassle. Perhaps the memory of the terrorists of 9/11 outweighs the inconvenience for many travelers.

FIGURE 11.9: TSA is Worth the Hassle

Yes	42.7%
No	24.9%
I don't know	32.3%

Source: BIGinsight.com

Summary

Since 9/11 what once was the strongest, most powerful nation in the world is now under siege by terrorists. The most powerful man in the world is not necessarily respected by all his fellow citizens. Congress isn't trusted. Government officials write malicious comments. To fly safely, we need a special organization to screen luggage and passengers.

Things just aren't turning out the way I thought they would when I was younger. Naively, I thought the bullying, teasing, and fights from the playground would stop after grade school. Little did I know the fights simply get more sophisticated as one ages.

Top five lessons learned

1. Consumers don't believe the recession is over.

2. Consumers' wealth is dropping due to declining home values, a fluctuating stock market decline, and lost jobs.

3. Consumers are disappointed and disgusted with Congress.

4. Consumers believe Julian Assange *and* the U.S. Government are to blame for leaked classified, unflattering information.

5. Many consumers (42.7% of those surveyed) believe the TSA is worth the inconvenience.

References

Alberts, Sheldon. "WikiLeaks Founder Urged to Stand Down." *National Post* (November 28, 2010) Retrieved March 32, 2011 from http://www.nationalpost.com/WikiLeaks+founder+urged+stand+down/3896103/story.html

Leonard, Peter and Robert Burns. "Clinton Says WikiLeaks Won't Hurt U.S. Diplomacy." Associated Press (December 1, 2010) Retrieved March 23, 2011 from http://www.signonsandiego.com/news/2010/dec/01/clinton-says-wikileaks-wont-hurt-us-diplomacy/

Chapter

12

Lessons Learned:
Where Do We Go From Here?

When I was young, my grandmother told me stories about the Great Depression of the 1930s. I didn't understand her pain of not knowing how to feed her family. She talked about the unemployment lines and the gratitude that her husband (my grandfather) was employed. I saw pictures but never really understood the gravity of the situation. I only remember hearing at the dinner table, "Be grateful, some families don't have anything to eat." So, I was grateful for the Brussels sprouts—I just held my nose when I was forced to eat them.

I loved my grandparents with all my heart and soul. We would watch movies about World War I and II. *Tora! Tora! Tora!* was and still is my all-time favorite movie. The film was based on real events, but for me it was just a movie. I could never truly comprehend the horror of the situation. September 11, 2001 changed all that. *Tora! Tora! Tora!* is still my favorite movie, but for an entirely different reason. Originally, I enjoyed the movie for the drama and historical perspective. Now, it is a reminder of the price of freedom.

The events of 9/11 changed the landscape of the United States. In many ways, it can be viewed as "Act One." During this act, Americans and consumers were taught to think and behave differently from the past. They became vigilant about security. They became more patriotic and grateful toward their country.

The recession of 2008 was not the result of terrorists, but it definitely was the "Act Two" to 9/11. In other words, the U.S. and its consumers were about to learn yet another series of very necessary lessons. These lessons were about fiscal responsibility, long-term financial planning, and placing needs above wants.

Act One and Act Two have revealed significant changes in the American consumer. Time will tell what happens in "Act Three." Act Three consists of implementing the lessons learned from consumers' responses. Fifty-five lessons have been identified through nationwide research and included in this book. Some of the lessons are common sense. Other lessons are enlightening. Regardless, the lessons can help businesses reach their target market. Gone are the days of simply selling a product or service. Businesses must identify with the needs and wants of the target market. The companies must then effectively communicate with the target market. The lessons learned will assist companies with that communication effort.

The New American Consumer

Chapter 1: Lessons Learned

1. The recession hit consumers hard, and only a quarter of consumers are confident about the economy.

2. Higher income wage earners worry more about being unemployed than do consumers earning less than $75,000 annually.

3. Most consumers are not prepared financially for the future.

4. Gone are the days of excess and satisfying our every desire. Consumers are thinking more about needs than wants.

5. Cash is king, debt is crippling, and credit will kill. An increased number of consumers are paying with cash.

Chapter 2: Lessons Learned

1. The weakened economy is influencing consumers to become more budget conscious.

2. Consumers appreciate credit cards—if one credit card is good, two is better. Visa is the most popular credit card.

3. There are many reasons consumers are motivated to use credit cards more often. The three top reasons are lower interest rates, cash back, and rewards or points programs.

4. Debt is a national way of life. Consumers' strive to pay down debt, while less than 30% intend to increase their savings.

5. Consumers are retiring later in life.

Chapter 3: Lessons Learned

1. The American dream for a castle is turning into an albatross around the necks of many.

2. "Security first" are the watchwords when looking for a home loan. Consumers are obtaining a fixed loan in order to keep financial stability in their lives.

3. More single consumers are purchasing a home than in the past.

4. Home equity loans are equal opportunity sources of additional income. Consumers with incomes under $75,000 are increasingly obtaining a second mortgage.

5. Consumers are divided regarding the U.S. government's involvement in helping save the housing market.

Chapter 4: Lessons Learned

1. Just because an industry is in the private sector doesn't mean the government won't get involved. The cash for clunkers program and the Toyota recall demonstrates the polar ends of the government's outreach to the automobile industry.

2. Vehicle preferences are changing rapidly. The once popular minivan is being replaced by other vehicles.

3. Vehicles possess definite personalities, and they are marketed toward specific genders and groups.

4. An SUV is popular by men and women.

5. The Congressional Hearings on the Toyota recall hurt the company as perceived by the consumer.

Chapter 5: Lessons Learned

1. Coupons are extremely popular and highly desired by consumers. Coupons build traffic, generate sales, and build store loyalty.

2. Consumers are purchasing increasingly more store brands in combination with national brands. Successful store brand merchandise is carried by Target, Kohl's, and JCPenney.

3. Fashion-oriented discount stores are attracting consumers in all household income brackets. Fashions by top designers at popular prices are bringing consumers into Kohl's.

4. The popularity of malls continues to decline. They are no longer the designated "hang out" for shoppers and teens. As gas prices increase, the number of trips to the mall decreases.

5. Men are becoming increasingly more active online shoppers.

Chapter 6: Lessons Learned

1. Consumers continue to eat fast food despite the calories, carbohydrates, sugar, and heavy advertising campaigns regarding their evils.

2. Men and women are equally prone to grab a burger, fries, and soda through a fast-food window. Neither sex has a reason to act superior when talking about their restraint from eating fast food.

3. Single people are the primary patrons of fast-food restaurants.

4. Fast-food advertisements may cater to young children, but the dominant consumer is over eighteen years old.

5. There is also a clear cut "winner" in terms of a favorite fast-food restaurant — McDonald's.

Chapter 7: Lessons Learned

1. Walmart and Target dominate in multiple categories as big box retailers.

2. The female customer is important to the hardware industry.

3. The demographics of the Lowe's and the Home Depot consumer are similar.

4. Toy big box retailers (Walmart, Toys "R" Us, Target) cater to different income brackets.

5. Best Buy consumers had a high average income ($62,023).

Chapter 8: Lessons Learned

1. Consumers who shop from home earn well above the national average income.

2. Catalog, TV, and online shoppers are young: in their thirties to early forties.

3. Over 40% of the consumers who shop at home are married.

4. Singles comprise 28–35% of consumers who shop at home.

5. Men are the dominant TV shopper.

Chapter 9: Lessons Learned

1. The three top reasons consumers 55 and older switch cell phone providers are: (a) coverage, (b) price, and (c) customer service.

2. The three most important attributes in a cell phone differ by age. In other words, cell phone providers would be wise to market phone attributes (such as text messaging, camera-enabled, or caller ID capabilities) based on the age of the target market.

3. Twitter is popular among stars as a promotional tool, but not heavily adopted by the majority of consumers.

4. The majority of Facebook users are aged 18–34 years old.

5. Consumers text family and friends about everything!

Chapter 10: Lessons Learned

1. More than 3/4th of the consumers surveyed are registered voters.

2. If the presidential election were held today, 38.5% would vote for someone other than President Obama.

3. Approximately 22% of all consumers and consumers earning $50,000 household income or more declare themselves as independents.

4. The majority of consumers surveyed are not confident about the nation's security.

5. The vast majority of consumers spend their tax refund by paying down debt or placing their money in savings.

Chapter 11: Lessons Learned

1. Consumers don't believe the recession is over.

2. Consumers' wealth is dropping due to declining home values, a fluctuating stock market decline, and lost jobs.

3. Consumers are disappointed and disgusted with Congress.

4. Consumers believe Julian Assange *and* the U.S. Government are to blame for leaked classified, unflattering information.

5. Many consumers (42.7% of those surveyed) believe the TSA is worth the inconvenience.

About the Authors

Marianne Bickle

Retail author, lecturer, researcher and consultant Dr. Marianne Bickle is the director of the Center for Retailing at the University of South Carolina. The center provides both local and international projects and research focusing on industry competiveness. Her industry and academic experiences with brick-and-mortar retailing, direct marketing and Internet retailing, provides her with clarity and insight into the dynamic retail environment.

Dr. Bickle has conducted research in cross-channel shopping behavior, internet shopping, social responsibility, fashion marketing, effectiveness of visual merchandising techniques, category management, and consumer behavior decision making in a tourism environment. Her professional work includes market analysis, survey research, corporate training, and participation on retail Board of Directors.

Dr. Bickle is the author of *Fashion Marketing: Theory, Principles and Practice* published by Fairchild Books. She blogs weekly for *Forbes* and has published and presented in excess of 90 peer refereed papers in relation to retailing. She is on the Board of Directors on a privately owned fashion company and is a regular retail contributing expert for news corporations.

The Prosper Foundation

The Prosper Foundation is a Not-for-Profit supporting entrepreneurship and innovation. It facilitates transdisciplinary collaboration using consumer insights as the common language. Founded in 1993 by Gary Drenik and Philip Rist, the Prosper Foundation currently provides information grants to 15 academic institutions. For more information please visit our website.

http://www.goprosper.com/prosperfoundation.html

Made in the USA
Charleston, SC
16 December 2013